Exploring Perception

A CD-ROM for Macintosh® and Microsoft® Windows®

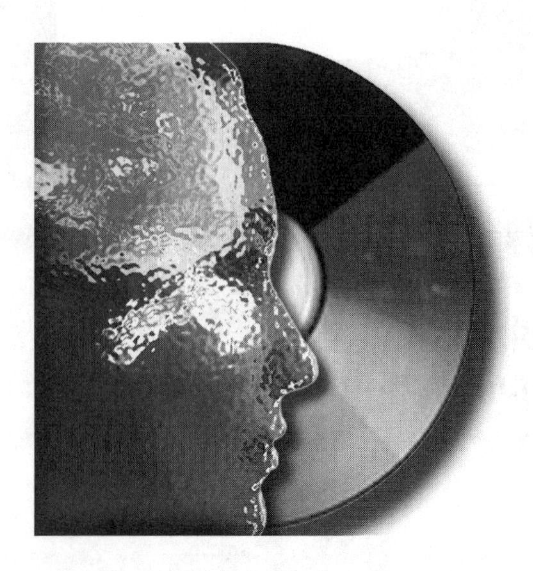

CD-ROM System Requirements

Macintosh®

Processor	68040 or later CPU, 33 MHz or better
System	System 7.1 or later
Monitor	640 × 480, 256 colors
RAM	16 MB recommended
CD-ROM	Minimum double-speed CD-ROM drive

PC

Processor	80486 or later CPU, 33 MHz or better
System	Microsoft® Windows® 3.0 or later
Monitor	640 × 480, 256 colors
RAM	16 MB recommended
CD-ROM	Minimum double-speed CD-ROM drive

Exploring Perception

A CD-ROM for Macintosh® and Microsoft® Windows®

Colin Ryan
James Cook University

Co-published by

Brooks/Cole Publishing Company

and

Nelson ITP

I(T)P® International Thomson Publishing Companies

Pacific Grove • Albany • Belmont • Bonn • Boston • Cincinnati • Detroit • Johannesburg • London
Madrid • Melbourne • Mexico City • New York • Paris • Singapore • Tokyo • Toronto • Washington

Sponsoring Editor: *Marianne Taflinger*
Marketing Team: *Marcy Perman, Christine Davis*
Editorial Assistant: *Scott Brearton*
Production Coordinator: *Marlene Thom*
Permissions Editor: *May Clark*
Manuscript Editor: *Lura Harrison*
Cover Design: *Vernon T. Boes*
Photo Editor: *Larry Molmud*
Typesetting: *Scratchgravel Publishing Services*
Printing and Binding: *Malloy Lithographing, Inc.*

For more information, contact:

BROOKS/COLE PUBLISHING COMPANY
511 Forest Lodge Road
Pacific Grove, CA 93950
USA

International Thomson Publishing Europe
Berkshire House 168–173
High Holborn
London WC1V 7AA
England

Nelson ITP
102 Dodds Street
South Melbourne, 3205
Victoria, Australia

Nelson Canada
1120 Birchmount Road
Scarborough, Ontario
Canada M1K 5G4

International Thomson Editores
Seneca 53
Col. Polanco
México, D. F., México
C. P. 11560

International Thomson Publishing GmbH
Königswinterer Strasse 418
53227 Bonn
Germany

International Thomson Publishing Asia
221 Henderson Road
#05–10 Henderson Building
Singapore 0315

International Thomson Publishing Japan
Hirakawacho Kyowa Building, 3F
2–2–1 Hirakawacho
Chiyoda-ku, Tokyo 102
Japan

Printed in the United States of America

10 9 8

ISBN 0-534-32104-6

Contents

UNIT GUIDES

Acknowledgments

This was my first foray into multimedia. *Exploring Perception* was a long journey on a challenging road in a strange land with few signposts. I was lucky indeed to have had such talented, farsighted, resourceful, and humane companions. I had much to learn and they taught me patiently and well. I learned, above all, that multimedia is the ultimate team sport.

Exploring Perception reflects the efforts, skills, and passions of many people. None played more constructive or enduring roles than Andrew Bruckshaw and Lawrence D'mello. We worked long hours together as the months became years. I sincerely thank them for all the nights, weekends, and holidays they gave up to see this project through. They did much more than might reasonably have been asked of them. *Exploring Perception* is a tribute to their craftsmanship, dedication, and extraordinary talents.

Andrew is a coding *virtuoso*. He has a rare gift. I thank him for his patience as I learned my craft and for his unwavering commitment to quality and excellence. By any standards, *Exploring Perception* was a vast programming challenge. Andrew carried an enormous, lone responsibility, and he delivered admirably.

Lawrence D'mello made a massive contribution to *Exploring Perception,* particularly to its look and feel: the bulk of the fine design and artwork is his. I thank him for his incredibly hard work and dedication and for his profound humanity and decency throughout the project. Lawrence's contribution to *Exploring Perception* goes far beyond his formidable graphic design, however. He shared the vision and commitment from the beginning and was a vital part of managing and delivering the project.

I am particularly grateful to Theo Prosenica, project manager, for his drive, imagination, and commitment. It was always much more than a job to Theo. His luminous belief in *Exploring Perception* buoyed me through some difficult times.

I must pay tribute to the people at Brooks/Cole in Pacific Grove, California. This project was a particular challenge for them, with an untried multimedia author beyond the Pacific—somewhere *Downunder*. Without exception, they were calm, reassuring, methodical, and totally professional.

Without the vision, astute support, and unflagging sense of purpose of Marianne Taflinger, *Exploring Perception*'s sponsoring editor, the project simply would not have happened. She has my sincere and lasting gratitude. The best I can hope for is that Marianne is proud of what we have done. May she have less cantankerous authors in the future.

My production editor, Marlene Thom, epitomized the best qualities of the Brooks/Cole team: she was totally professional; always prompt and purposeful; and very, very, good at her job. I envy her subtlety and grace: it is a rare skill to beguile a vain and crusty author into actually enjoying criticism. Permissions editor May Clark organized the necessary authorizations with care and skill and led me patiently and kindly through the permissions process.

Bob Beede, multimedia specialist at Brooks/Cole, was a valuable source of advice and practical guidance throughout the project. Bob's sense of the worth of the enterprise was always encouraging, and his meticulous oversight of the complex voice-over production process was a major contribution.

Scott Brearton, editorial assistant to Marianne Taflinger, handled my many requests for information and assistance with crisp efficiency and coordinated the several rounds of reviews meticulously.

The clear, calm voice that runs throughout *Exploring Perception* like a silken thread belongs to Paula Bliss. Voice-over recording was carried out assiduously by Animation Farm, and I am grateful to them both for their excellent contributions.

I would like to record my thanks to Thomas Nelson Australia, who bravely and farsightedly sponsored a complex and expensive project and saw it through to completion. Tony Palmer made a significant contribution to setting the initial design parameters and his quiet, wry humor and formidable talents served the project well in its formative phases. Acquisitions editor Julie McNab forged the partnership between TNA and Brooks/Cole that made *Exploring Perception* possible.

Professor E. Bruce Goldstein of the University of Pittsburgh was involved in the project from the early conceptual stages and consulted constantly, right through to completion. Bruce was a terrific source of encouragement and advice as our original idea crystallized, and his monumental expertise in sensation and perception has been invaluable. I thank him for the countless hours he lavished on the project. Bruce also kindly allowed me to make liberal use of the resources of his excellent text *Sensation and Perception*. I'm delighted that Brooks/Cole will be offering *Exploring Perception* with Bruce Goldstein's text.

Exploring Perception owes a great debt to the numerous reviewers who commented in detail on the scripts and the CD at every stage of the long and arduous development process. I cannot overstate the importance of their contribution. Without their personal generosity, compendious knowledge, and diligence, *Exploring Perception* would be greatly diminished. Ultimate responsibility for any errors and omissions is wholly mine, of course. In particular, my heartfelt thanks go to:

Richard Abrams, Washington University
Deborah Aks, University of Wisconsin–Whitewater
Frank M. Bagrash, California State University at Fullerton
Michael Biderman, University of Tennessee–Chattanooga
Greg Bohemier, Culver-Stockton College
Richard Bowen, Loyola University
Gregory Burton, Seton Hall University
Alan Davis, Montana State University
E. Bruce Goldstein, University of Pittsburgh
Morton A. Heller, Winston-Salem State University
Glen Meyer, Trinity University
Paul Schulman, State University of New York–Marcy
Jim Sheridan, Millersville University
Steven K. Shevell, University of Chicago
Kenneth Short, Creighton University
Michael Stoloff, James Madison University
Benjamin Wallace, Cleveland State University
Peter Wenderoth, Macquarie University
David Williams, University of Rochester
Steven Yantis, The Johns Hopkins University

Some years ago Professor Barbara Gillam kindly offered me the hospitality of her laboratory at the University of New South Wales and encouraged me to begin *exploring perception*. In so doing, she started me on a fascinating journey and inadvertently sowed the seeds of this project. Barbara's humanity and shining intellect are a continuing inspiration.

I must also acknowledge the constructive encouragement and support the project received from James Cook University of North Queensland, particularly in the crucial early stages of the project, not least from its Research Administration. Jenna Clark deserves special mention in this regard. I also want to acknowledge the contribution of Professor J. Michael Innes, then Head of the Department of Psychology and Sociology at JCU. It is difficult to overstate the importance of Mike's imaginative and timely financial support.

Several other colleagues and students at James Cook University made significant material and intellectual contributions, for which I sincerely thank them: David Mitchell, Michael Smithson, Sam Huf, Nicole Leslie, and Bruce Young, in particular. Special thanks must go to the assiduous and always affable Fiona Fidler and Tim Lockard, who provided invaluable assistance with the Readings and Glossary and scaled a mountain of testing and checking. Thanks also to my talented and good-natured undergraduate sensation and perception students at JCU, who graciously allowed me to practice on them and who provided invaluable feedback on early prototypes of the CD material.

I should also acknowledge the work of Alan Nimmo of the Department of Physiology and Pharmacology at JCU, who made a significant conceptual contribution when the project was being developed and materially influenced the content of Module 1. Karl Eastwood was responsible for much of the design and illustration of that module. He carried out a complex and demanding task with skill, flair, and diligence.

Exploring Perception owes its major debt, of course, to the generations of scholars who have brought us to this point in our understanding of sensation and perception. Time and again while researching this project, I have stopped to marvel—literally, to gape—at their ingenuity, insight, and just plain genius. In a very real sense, *Exploring Perception* is their work, not mine.

Each evening, the *MV Islander IV* lurches into the tropic sea, taking us home to the granite and hoop pine of Magnetic Island. There is a small group of us who sit out in the open air, upstairs, behind the wheelhouse. The beer is cold, the company is good, and the conversation is always revivifying. I want to thank those fine companions, who endured my arcane enthusiasms, jollied me when the task seemed endless and best of all were just, irrepressibly and remorselessly, themselves. They played a more sustaining role in *Exploring Perception* than they ever knew.

Finally, I must thank my wife, fond companion, and gifted colleague, Janet Greeley, for her encouragement, understanding, equanimity, and excellent professional advice over the years it took to bring this project to fruition. *Exploring Perception* is dedicated to Janet.

Preface

The recent emergence of widely available CD-ROM storage technology, and a new generation of sophisticated software authoring tools, have paved the way for extraordinary developments in interactive multimedia. Those developments have sown the seeds of a revolution in education that is rapidly gaining momentum; the way we learn and the way we teach will never be quite the same again.

In psychology, these new technologies are making possible the cost-effective realization of hands-on, computer-based, classroom exploration of complex psychological and physiological phenomena. Few areas of the discipline lend themselves to the new technology as readily as human sensation and perception.

In this first phase of *Exploring Perception*, I have focused on the *classic* perceptual phenomena that are dealt with, directly or indirectly, in most perception texts. It has been developed to dovetail with, and complement, those texts, capitalizing on their formidable strengths. Thus, I have strongly encouraged students to attach their CD interactive experiences to the solid, systematic, intellectual backbone of the discipline by providing detailed on-board page references to several key texts throughout. This is recognition of the fact that there are many things that printed texts do—and will continue to do—uniquely well.

In designing and constructing *Exploring Perception* we have tried to avoid producing a *talking book*. For this reason, its structure is wholly modular, rather than linear and cumulative; and commentary and on-screen text have been kept to a minimum. Our aim has been to set the scene, give users an interesting set of tools, then encourage them to explore each phenomenon in their own way, at their own speed. Ideally, I wanted you to be able to *graze* the material at will, rather than be tyrannized by a predetermined linear path. A major challenge has been to retain the liberating virtues of a modular structure while maintaining a reasonable degree of coherence and focus. This has led us to provide this short, bridging, companion handbook to complement the core texts around which *Exploring Perception* is built.

Many universities and colleges are only just beginning to develop dedicated multimedia classrooms. Presently, few have group facilities that allow for individual listening in sound-isolated booths, or via headsets. We made the difficult strategic decision that, although this first volume of *Exploring Perception* would have a voice-over commentary, it would be usable in its entirety with the sound switched off. Although this restriction makes the package suitable for use in virtually all classroom settings, it necessarily has limited the scope of the material that could be included in this package—a situation we hope to remedy as more dedicated multimedia classrooms are developed.

This Handbook

This short volume provides an overview of the *Exploring Perception* CD. In addition to providing instructions and guidelines for using the CD, it contains 40 brief, scene-setting introductions to the units into which the concept explorations, or interactions, are grouped. These notes, or sketches, are intended to provide no more than some quick, colloquial, context for the interactions that make up each unit. They flag important issues in each and (I hope) will guide the way in which users approach an interaction, influencing what they seek and find in each.

These unit-level summaries will sometimes add the caveats, clarification, cautionary notes, hints for further reading, or interesting asides precluded by the rather restrictive format of the CD material. I hope they will quickly make clear to the user what each unit, as a whole, is driving at and where it fits in the module of which it is part.

I should make very clear that this modest handbook is not a textbook, a textbook-surrogate, or even a minitext. Advanced students will need to have a more detailed knowledge and understanding of the concepts explored than is provided by the CD and this short companion volume taken together. As already noted, detailed page references to some of the major texts in this area are provided with each interaction for that reason. You will be systematically guided to primary sources by those texts. Accordingly, I have kept the citation of primary sources to an absolute minimum in the body of this handbook. Our aim has been to provide a quick, accessible, informal, scene-setting primer geared specifically to the CD material. Both CD and handbook are intended, then, to be useful complements to the core texts, not an effort to duplicate what they already do very well.

Referenced Texts

You will find in every interaction detailed page references to some, or all, of seven major texts.

Coren, S., Ward, L. M., & Enns, J. T. (1994). *Sensation and perception* (4th ed.). Orlando, FL: Harcourt Brace.

Goldstein, E. B. (1996). *Sensation and perception* (4th ed.). Pacific Grove, CA: Brooks/Cole.

Graham, R. B. (1990). *Physiological psychology*. Belmont, CA: Wadsworth.

Kalat, J. W. (1995). *Biological psychology* (5th ed.). Pacific Grove, CA: Brooks/Cole.

Matlin, M. W., & Foley, H. J. (1992). *Sensation and perception* (3rd ed.). Needham Heights, MA: Allyn and Bacon.

Schiffman, H. R. (1996). *Sensation and perception: An integrated approach* (4th ed.). New York: John Wiley & Sons.

Sekuler, R., & Blake, R. (1994) *Perception* (3rd ed.). New York: McGraw-Hill.

These books (each, without exception, excellent) point students to the vital primary sources; provide useful summary and preview materials; pose much more subtle and challenging quiz questions than the interaction-specific CD quizzes allow; and provide wonderful enrichment, integration, and depth. They all provide the systematic, linear development of ideas and concepts that the deliberately modular, "free-range" or "grazing," approach of the *Exploring Perception* CD—with its self-contained, standalone interactions—does not afford. *Exploring Perception* complements those texts. It certainly cannot replace them. Indeed, it owes a substantial debt to all of them.

Where I have listed a text and cited specific page numbers in the Readings section embedded in each interaction Text box, I have typically drawn on that source in framing and distilling the ideas explored. This should be taken as acknowledgment of my substantial intellectual debt to those authors. Without their remarkable, systematic contributions, *Exploring Perception* would have remained the mere shadow of an idea.

I would be delighted to hear from users of the package. Your questions, comments, suggestions, and corrections would be most welcome. Please feel free to e-mail me: Colin.Ryan@jcu.edu.au.

Colin Ryan

Structure of the CD

As noted, *Exploring Perception* is wholly modular. It consists of 240 concept explorations, or *interactions*, grouped into 40 thematic sequences, or *units*. Those units are organized into five *modules* representing major content areas common to most perception courses. The emphasis is on flexibility: there is no predetermined path through the package.

Interactions usually are designed as standalone explorations of a single concept or phenomenon. As such, they can be investigated in any order. Although there is usually some progression from easier to harder concepts within a unit, users should be able to understand the essential point made by each interaction without having done particular, preceding interactions.

Exploring Perception encourages a grazing style of go-anywhere exploration. Users do not have to begin at the beginning and work through to the end. Thus, it is possible to skip from unit to unit—even shift modules—at any time, essentially without cost. The *Organizer* facility allows you to check (or tick) successfully completed interactions and store a record your activity over many sessions; so keeping track of where you are is made quite simple.

We have consciously eschewed making cross references among interactions to avoid externally driving student exploration. Instead, we hope that thematic grouping of similar interactions into units—and, ultimately, into modules—will serve to guide students who feel they need it without tyrannizing those who don't. So, quite deliberately, there is no preordained path.

The thematic organization of the modular CD material provides some structure and context, but users will need to work through the readings keyed to each interaction to truly understand and integrate the experiences and insights that *Exploring Perception* provides. The unit-level summaries provided in this short handbook should also help make clear where each interaction fits in the broader conceptual scheme of things. So, to the extent that the simple modular format used precludes detailed theoretical development of the concepts investigated, users should read widely to augment their understanding.

A Note to Students

As you become familiar with *Exploring Perception*, you will use it in the way that best suits *your* needs, temperament, and learning style. That is as it should be! Some of you will probably read the appropriate Unit Guide in this handbook, then plunge right into the CD—with a textbook at your elbow just in case you need to check some things along the way—and later relate what you have seen and done to the "big picture" provided by a detailed reading of your textbook.

Others might want to read the text resources referenced with each interaction as they go—immediately cementing in place the insights they have gained—or leave all that until a second, revision, pass through the material. Some of my students like to read at least one of the key textbook chapters beforehand, and then occasionally refer to the Unit Guide, for clarification or direction, as they work through the interactions. As far as I can tell, there is no single *best way*. Experiment. See what suits you best.

Whichever approach you take, I hope you will find *Exploring Perception* friendly, engaging, forgiving, and fun. Each interaction is, in effect, self-contained. Each should be meaningful and leave you with a clear message, even if you just plunge straight into it out of the blue. Graze. And enjoy it.

CD Quizzes

I would encourage you to do the short quizzes embedded in each interaction as you go. They are usually fairly simple and address only the concepts explored in that interaction. They are intended to check that you have understood the main message, or observed what was intended. You will sometimes want, or need, to return to the interaction (to rework it) to check out an answer.

The quizzes are not intended to be a substitute for working through the exercises and the much more powerful and subtle revision questions in your text. Those text resources are typically more complex and are usually designed to assess whether you have understood, assimilated, and integrated the material presented. They usually check, also, whether you can apply that knowledge creatively. The quizzes in *Exploring Perception* are more *procedural* in nature, being designed to direct and tune what you observe. They highlight features of the interaction that are important and check that you have worked through the material as intended. In this sense, you will need to know much more about a topic than the CD quizzes typically will test.

Primary Sources

As noted, *Exploring Perception* has been designed to complement your textbook, not to replace it. It targets a set of core concepts, principles, and demonstrations—many of which appear, in one form or another, in mainstream texts—and seeks to make them accessible in the interesting, engaging, and hopefully enlightening ways made possible by the CD-ROM technology.

So, we have not sought to duplicate the texts, or their functions, but to augment and supplement them. It is important to note that *Exploring Perception* does not provide you with extensive lists of primary sources; you will find these in your textbooks (to which I refer you) and in the standard computer databases (for example, PsycLit). You will need to consult them and that will be an exciting enterprise—they are the wellspring of our science. It is vitally important that, with the guidance and advice of your teachers, you search out and digest the original research papers, not simply settle for the limited (but hopefully enjoyable and instructive) experience *Exploring Perception* provides.

A Note to Instructors

Perception is chock full of enough curiosities, paradoxes, and wonders to beguile even the most world-weary and obsidian-eyed, but teaching it can be a challenging business. The logistics of providing students with demonstrations of the main perceptual phenomena are particularly daunting, as all of us will attest who have fumbled with out-of-sequence overhead transparencies; miskeyed seven-digit frame numbers into laser disc players on the fly; or spent 3 hours wiring-up a classroom demonstration that self-destructs at the moment of truth. I hope *Exploring Perception* will go at least some way toward making our task a little easier, more efficient, and more enjoyable.

The Organizer and Lecture-Building

At James Cook University, which has good facilities for overhead projection of computer-generated images, I have begun to use *Exploring Perception* to provide interactive illustration of key principles in lectures. Although I encourage student participation in these lecture settings, the opportunities for meaningful, hands-on, individual exploration clearly are limited. So, that experience is supplemented with weekly workshop sessions in which students work through the material, coming together near the end of the session to review and discuss the phenomena they have encountered.

Exploring Perception has a simple structure and a convenient navigation system, but you might wish to demonstrate, in a particular lecture, material from several different modules. This is not too difficult to do using the standard navigation tools, but navigating a multimedia package in mid-lecture can be an undesirable distraction.

The on-board Organizer facility allows you to select a sequence of interactions in advance, then play them in a lecture with no additional navigation requirement. Once you have defined the sequence you want, you simply press the right-arrow key on the keyboard to move on to the next interaction. Press the left-arrow key to return to an earlier interaction—as you would in a simple slide show. It should take only about 5 minutes to learn how use the Organizer. Full details of Organizer features and operation are given in the Tutorial and later in this handbook.

Workshopping *Exploring Perception*

At JCU, weekly workshop sessions have replaced some tutorials and laboratory classes. These provide all students with the opportunity to explore selected material individually, with the instructor present to guide, advise, and assist them. Because many interactions entail quite extensive data gathering and analysis, the workshops complement our usual laboratory program, rather than detract from it. In particular, the hardwired data gathering interactions in the psychophysics module (Module 5)—with their strong emphasis on the mechanics of the classical psychophysical methods—provide an excellent introduction to later laboratory exercises. At a personal level, I have found this workshop format a very satisfying way to teach.

Voice-over Commentary: On Or Off?

Exploring Perception gives the option of using a voice-over commentary, which sets the scene for each interaction, or operating the CD with the sound switched off. In lecture settings, in particular, many instructors will choose to provide the context, or background, for a given exploration themselves. Many instructors also will find it preferable to operate with the sound switched off in cramped workshop settings, thus minimizing distraction to students from nearby neighbors working on different interactions.

A verbatim text of the voice-over commentary for any interaction is available at any time. This means that students working independently in a setting that precludes the use of the voice-over nevertheless have access to the background information provided by the commentary.

The text version of the commentary can be accessed, of course, even when the voice-over mode is being used. Some students have found it helps to consolidate the material, making note-taking a little easier, in both lectures and workshops.

Getting Started

Before You Begin

- Insert the CD into the CD-ROM player.
- Close all applications running in the background.
- Disable virtual memory.
- Insert a disk into the disk drive. Ensure it is formatted. Name the disk EPDISK. When that is done, copy the file EPPREFS.TXT to that disk from the Extras directory on the CD.

Place the same EPDISK in the disk drive each time you run *Exploring Perception* and click the Update button on the Modules menu screen. This will enable you to keep track of the interactions you have completed. At the end of each session, a record of the interactions you have completed successfully will be written to disk.

To Run *Exploring Perception*

Macintosh

When you have inserted the CD into the drive, the CD icon will appear on-screen. Double-click on that icon and then double-click on the EPMAC icon.

Windows

When you have inserted the CD into the drive, the CD icon will appear on-screen. Double-click on that icon and then double-click on the EPWIN icon.

CD Functions and Features at a Glance

Shell Functions

Exploring Perception provides a constant working environment, or shell, in which all interactive explorations are set. That shell provides six fixed functions that always appear in the blue band at the top of the screen. They can be accessed at any time. A further three context-sensitive, menu-related functions (Modules, Units, and Interactions) can be accessed where appropriate.

Tutorial A quick, directed tour of the functions and features of the *Exploring Perception* CD is available. Simply click **Tutorial** and follow the instructions. Clicking **Tutorial** a second time terminates the tutorial and returns you to your previous location in the program.

Credits For information about the author, publishers, software producer and all the people who made *Exploring Perception* possible, select **Credits** from the blue band. This will open a menu. Select from the available options. Click **Credits** again to close the window and return to your previous location in the program. Photo and figure credits are also provided here.

Sound You can adjust the volume of the voice-over commentary or, if you prefer, switch the sound off entirely. Click **Sound** to access the volume control, a pop-down volume control slider. To adjust the volume, click and drag the cursor to the desired setting. The sound may be turned off by setting the volume slider to 0. Click **Sound** again to hide the slider after use.

Organizer You will find the Organizer a powerful, but simple, tool. Simply click to open it. It does several useful things. First, it provides a hierarchically structured one-screen map of the entire contents of the CD. Second, it keeps a visible record of interactions successfully completed; you can tell at a glance what remains to be done. Third, the Organizer can be used to sequence and play a series of interactions without the need to navigate using the menus. You can define a sequence by clicking on the units or interactions you want, and then step back-and-forth through it using only the right-arrow and left-arrow keys. Sequences set up in advance are saved to disk when you quit the program and can be retrieved from disk at start-up using the Update facility. Finally, the Organizer can be used to list the contents of any unit or mod-

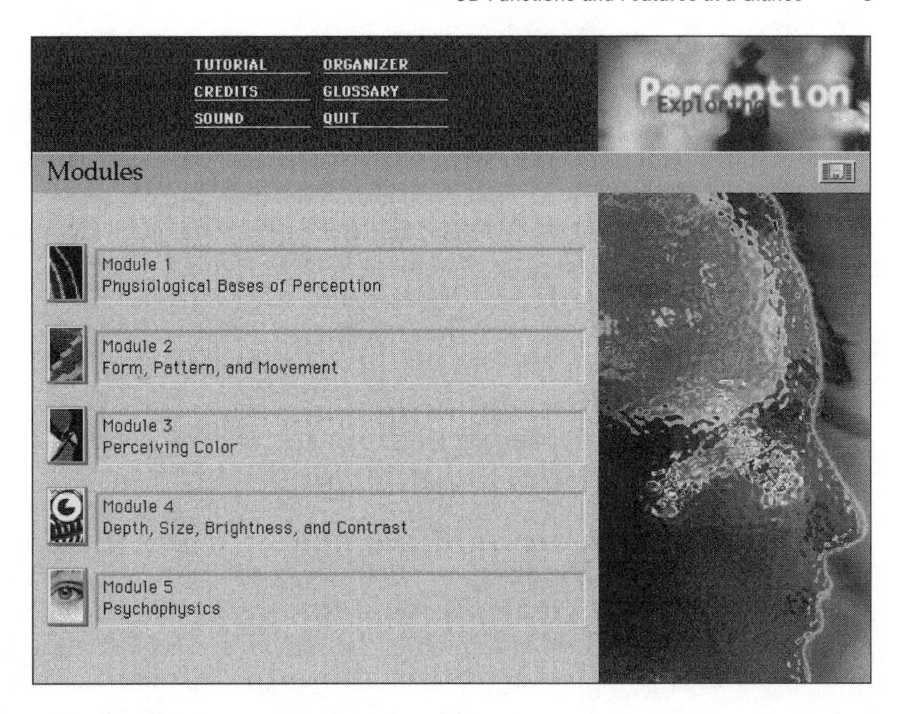

ule. Clicking **Organizer** a second time exits the Organizer and returns you to your previous location in the program

Glossary Occasionally, you may be unsure of the precise meaning of a technical term encountered in the commentary or on-screen text. To check the definition of problematic key words or phrases, click **Glossary**, and then select the first letter in the target word or phrase. You will then see a scroll-down list from which you select the targeted term. Click on that word or phrase to see its definition. Clicking **Glossary** a second time exits the Glossary and returns you to your previous location in the program.

Quit To exit the program at any time, click **Quit**. If you have selected, but not executed, a sequence of interactions using the Organizer, it will be saved to EPDISK automatically (provided it is in the floppy disk drive). In the same way, the record of interactions you have completed will be updated also.

Modules *Exploring Perception* contains five numbered modules, each with a distinctive graphic icon. The menu of available modules appears on the opening screen, shown above. A module can be selected for exploration by single-clicking the icon button adjacent to it. If you are not on the opening Modules menu screen, selecting the **Modules** function will take you directly to it. This option is not available in the blue band at the top of the screen if you are already in the Modules menu.

Units You can go directly to the menu of the units in the currently selected (active) module by selecting **Units** from the blue band at the top of the screen, or by selecting a module from the Modules menu. Each module contains eight units. Any of those units can be selected from the menu by single-clicking the button adjacent to it. This takes you to the Interactions menu for that unit. The **Units** option is not available in the blue band at the top of the screen if you are in the Modules or Units menus.

Interactions Each unit consists of six conceptually related interactions, or explorations. You can go directly to a menu of the interactions in the currently selected (active) unit by selecting **Interactions** from the blue band at the top of the screen, or by selecting any unit from the Units menu by clicking the button adjacent to it. If you are already in the Module, Units, or Interactions menus, this option is deleted from the blue band at the top of the screen.

Interaction-Specific Functions

As you work through the interactions, you will notice a row of four function buttons at the right end of the title band. They provide a range of additional interaction-specific functions and facilities:

Click this button when you have completed the currently active interaction to your satisfaction. The active interaction is thereby flagged with a check mark in the Organizer and in the Interactions matrix at the top right of the screen. This provides a convenient way of keeping track of your activity.

Click this button to replay the voice-over commentary for the currently active interaction. This can be done at any time.

Click this button for a verbatim text of the voice-over commentary for the currently active interaction. It will appear in a *Text* box at the center of the screen. This feature provides access to the background information given by the voice-over when the sound is switched off. Click a second time to close the *Text* box. The *Text* box will close automatically if you open the *Quiz* box or exit the interaction.

Click this button to access the quiz for the active interaction. A *Quiz* box will open at the center of the screen containing a set of interaction-specific questions. Each *Quiz* box has one, two, or three buttons at the top-right, indicating that one, two, or three questions are available for that interaction. Select the question you want by clicking the appropriate button. Click a second time to close the *Quiz* box. The *Quiz* box will close automatically if you open the *Text* box or exit the interaction.

Auxiliary Functions

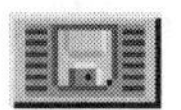

Update If you quit *Exploring Perception* with your personal floppy disk (EPDISK) installed in the disk drive, any defined (but unused) sequence of interactions is automatically saved to that disk. A record of successfully completed interactions (those you have placed a check mark against in the Interactions matrix) is also saved. When next you restart the package you should ensure EPDISK is again in the drive, and immediately click the Update button on the Modules menu, which always appears after the opening titles. This will cause the program to automatically update your activity record in the Organizer and the Interactions matrix for each unit. It will also load any saved sequence of interactions into the Sequence window of the Organizer.

Run This button is located at the top-right of the Organizer screen. Clicking on it will run the sequence of interactions defined in the Sequence window of the Organizer, beginning with the first interaction (bottom-most in the Sequence window). Having initiated the sequence in this way, you can step backward and forward through it using the left- and right-arrow keys on your computer keyboard, respectively.

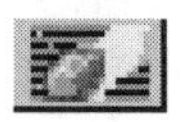

Clear This button is also located at the top-right of the Organizer screen. Clicking on it will clear the contents of the Sequence window of the Organizer.

Interactions Matrix

At the top-right corner of the screen is a 2 x 3 matrix of keys or buttons. This matrix provides a convenient way of navigating the six interactions

in the currently selected unit without repeatedly having to return to the Interactions menu. In line with the "grazing" philosophy of the package, clicking one of the six keys will take you directly to the interaction it represents. The matrix keys are not numbered (deliberately!), but you will quickly realize they run from top-left to bottom-right: the first interaction in the current unit is at top-left, the sixth is at bottom-right.

Using the Organizer

Organizer Features

The Organizer is a powerful and flexible tool for sequencing and tracking your use of the modularly organized material on the CD. It provides:

- A hierarchically structured one-screen map of the entire contents of *Exploring Perception*
- A visible record of interactions successfully completed; you can tell at a glance what remains to be done
- The ability to sequence and run a series of interactions without needing to navigate around the package using menus
- An immediate listing of the contents of any selected unit or module

Click on the Shell function **Organizer** to activate it.

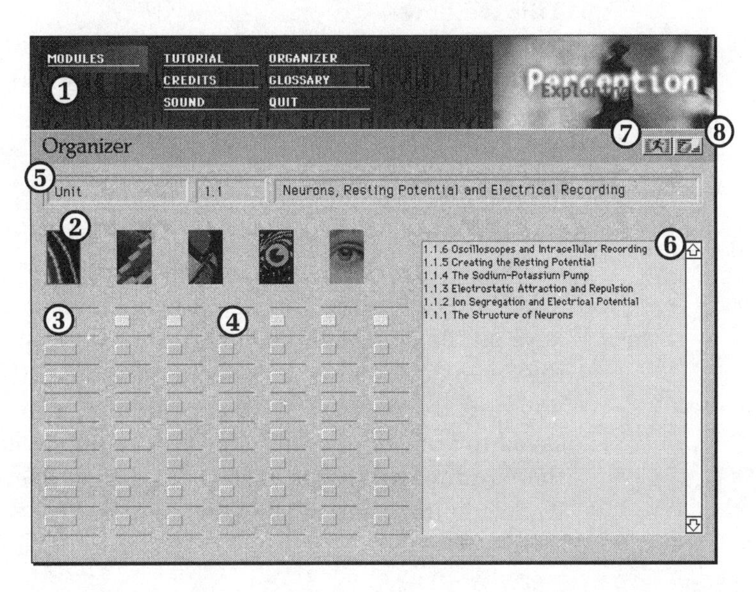

The Organizer Screen

The Organizer screen consists of:

1. **The shell**
   This provides you with ready access to the nine functions and features previously discussed.

2. **Module icons**
   Each of the five modules has a distinctive graphic icon. Running the mouse arrow over an icon, or pointing to it, highlights the icon; defines the corresponding module as the active module; and displays the module title in the *Title* window (5).

3. **Units keys**
   This column of eight rectangular keys represents the eight units in the active module. When you *point* to any unit key, the number and title of the corresponding unit appears in the *Title* window. Clicking any unit key adds the six interactions in that unit to the *Sequence* window (6). Clicking again deletes them.

4. **Interaction keys**
   Each row of six keys corresponds to the six interactions in a unit. When you point to any interaction key, the number and title of the corresponding interaction appears in the *Title* window. Clicking any interaction key adds that interaction to the *Sequence* window. Clicking again deletes that interaction from the defined sequence.

5. **Title window**
   This window contains the number and title of the module, unit, or interaction to which the mouse arrow is pointing—that is, the active module, unit, or interaction.

6. **Sequence window**
   The *Sequence* window contains the list of interactions you have defined. To initiate that sequence of interactions click the *Run* key (7). Once a sequence of interactions is initiated, you can step serially backward or forward through it using the left-arrow and right-arrow keys on the computer keyboard, respectively. Enter interactions in the *Sequence* window by selecting the desired unit or interaction. If you quit the package with a sequence in this window, it will be saved to your floppy disk (EPDISK) automatically and reentered in the window when you restart *Exploring Perception* and click the Update button with EPDISK in the drive.

7. **Run key**
   Clicking this key initiates or runs the defined sequence of interactions currently in the *Sequence* window.

8. **Clear key**
   Clicking this key clears the contents of the *Sequence* window.

Quick Guide to Organizer Functions

How To

- **Identify any module, unit, or interaction**

Point to the target module icon, unit key, or interaction key with the mouse arrow. Its name and identifying number will appear in the *Title* window.

- **List the interactions in a unit**

Click on the appropriate unit key. The interactions in that unit will be listed in the *Sequence* window. You can list the contents of several units in this way. To clear lists, click once on the *Clear* key.

- **Define a sequence of interactions**

Click on the required units or interactions in the order you want to use them. They will be added automatically to the *Sequence* window, with the last selected interaction listed first. If you select an entire unit, the interactions in that unit will be added to the list in the window, in descending order.

- **Run the sequence of interactions you have defined**

Click the *Run* key. This will take you to the first interaction in your defined sequence. Once a sequence is initiated, you can step serially backward or forward through the interactions using the left-arrow and right-arrow keys on the computer keyboard, respectively. There is no need to navigate to each interaction using the menus. Instructors may find this sequencing feature useful in building lectures or workshop sessions in advance—obviating the need to navigate the package on the fly—whereas students may find it more convenient to specify a sequence of concept explorations in advance and then simply step through them.

- **Save a sequence of interactions for later use**

To save a sequence for later use, simply ensure your floppy disk (EPDISK) is in the disk drive at the time you quit *Exploring Perception.*

Any sequence in the *Sequence* window that has not been run will be automatically saved to the disk when you quit. Provided that disk is in the drive when you restart *Exploring Perception* and click the Update button, the sequence will be automatically reloaded into the *Sequence* window, ready to be run.

- **Clear a sequence of interactions from the window**

To clear a sequence simply click the *Clear* key.

- **Keep track of completed interactions**

Keep track of interactions completed to your satisfaction by clicking the ✓ key as you finish each one. This inserts a check mark in the appropriate cell in the Interactions matrix as well as one in the map of contents in the Organizer. When you **Quit** each session, this history is automatically saved to your EPDISK floppy and the Organizer is automatically updated when you next start *Exploring Perception,* provided your EPDISK is in the drive and you click the Update button at the beginning of the session.

- **Erase check marks from the Organizer**

Your history of successfully completed interactions is stored on EPDISK and continually updated. To erase that history, simply delete all files on that disk except EPPREFS.TXT. All check marks in the Organizer will be deleted. The EPDISK disk can then be reused.

UNIT GUIDES

Module 1

Physiological Bases of Perception

Unit 1.1 Neurons, Electrochemistry, and Intracellular Recording

Nerve cells, or neurons, are the building blocks—the basic functional units—of the nervous system, generating, receiving, and transmitting information in the form of electrical signals. It is important that you understand their basic structure and function, and something of the way in which they interact. Although neurons vary widely in gross physical structure, their elements are similar and we can usefully generalize. The illustrations of neurons used in this module are, then, convenient idealizations and you should not take them too literally. An image of actual neural tissue, greatly magnified, can be found in **Interaction 1.1.6**; it will help you appreciate the way neurons look in reality. You also will find several illustrations of different types of neurons in the core texts.

A typical sensory system is a string of neurons, stretching from a receptor to the brain. Receptors are simply specialized constellations of neurons. Axon and dendrite fibers, or processes, may extend from a few microns (one-millionth of a meter) to several feet in length—extending from (say) the base of the spine to the tip of the big toe. The diameters of these processes are microscopic, varying from approximately 1 to 20 microns. There is no guarantee a particular signal leaving the receptor will arrive at the cortex because it must traverse many synapses, where it may encounter inhibitory as well as excitatory inputs. Some neurons receive inputs from thousands of other neurons.

In this unit you will be able to explore the structure and function of both motor and sensory neurons and simulate the process of firing them (**Interaction 1.1.1**). Excitation arriving at the neuron via the dendrites is called an *afferent* impulse. Excitation exiting through the axon and telodendrites is called an *efferent* impulse. You will encounter this distinction quite often, so be sure you know which is which.

Unit 1.2 explores the generation and transmission of information in neurons in some detail. You will regularly encounter references to the electrostatic forces of attraction and repulsion between ions, and to the sodium-potassium pump, both of which play vital roles in preparing cells to fire. You will find it helpful to have an elementary understanding of the processes involved in each before moving on to the more complex interactions dealing with resting potentials and action potentials.

First, you will need a little electrochemistry and **Interaction 1.1.2** allows you to explore some simple, but important, concepts. Atoms or molecules typically are in electrostatic equilibrium—that is, the number of negatively charged electrons is equal to the number of positively charged protons. They may, however, gain or lose one or more electrons, resulting in a net negative or positive electrostatic charge, respectively. These charged particles are called *ions* and play a vital role in the transmission of signals in the nervous system.

All neurons are covered by a very thin, porous membrane that controls the exchange of chemicals (including charged ions) between the inside and outside of the cell. If the membrane effectively segregates positively and negatively charged ions, a difference in voltage—an electrical potential—is set up between the inside and the outside of the cell.

In Interaction 1.1.2, you can explore the role ion segregation plays in creating an electrical potential. In effect, you can vary the segregation of the ions (charges) and note the impact on the electrical potential (measured in volts) between the two compartments of a cell. The differences in potential in a living neuron are tiny. They are usually expressed in millivolts (thousandths of a volt).

It is very important that you comprehend the meaning of *polarization* and *depolarization* discussed in Interaction 1.1.2. These are critical concepts in understanding the generation and transmission of neural signals and will be encountered often. You can think of polarization as the progressive segregation from each other of ions of different charge. Polarization is reflected in an increase in electrical potential. Depolarization, on the other hand, is the progressive desegregation, or mixing, of ions of different charge. It is reflected in a decrease in electrical potential.

The key point to take away from **Interaction 1.1.3** is simply that ions of like (identical) charge repel each other, whereas ions of dissimilar charge attract. Thus, two positively charged ions will repel each other. So will two negatively charged ions. Positive and negative ions, in contrast, attract each other. This is important for our purposes because these electrostatic forces play a crucial role in determining the distribution of ions inside and outside the cell which, in turn, is a critical factor in determining the responsivity of the cell to stimulation.

After a cell has fired or signaled—after an action potential has occurred—it is necessary to restore and maintain the chemical (ion) balance, so that the cell is readied to fire again. In general terms, this will require that there be more potassium ions inside the cell than out, and a predominance of sodium ions outside the cell. The sodium-potassium pump plays an important role in this process. In essence, it pumps three sodium ions out of the cell for every two potassium ions it pumps in. You will probably need only to know the general principle explored in **Interaction 1.1.4**. The sodium-potassium pump is really a sophisticated protein and not a mechanical pump, as such. So, again, don't be too literal here.

You may find **Interaction 1.1.5** rather difficult. It encapsulates a number of very important, but complex, ideas. Persevere! If you master this interaction you will be well on your way to understanding the processes that, together, result in the resting potential—and the resting potential is the wellspring from which all neural activity derives. If you are working sequentially through this unit, you already will have encountered some of the processes at work: electrostatic attraction and repulsion and the sodium-potassium pump.

We can record the electrical activity taking place within a cell using a tiny microelectrode inserted into it. This kind of intracellular recording of electrical activity has revealed a great deal about the operation of the nervous system. In **Interaction 1.1.6**, you can simulate inserting a microelectrode and observing a cell's activity using an oscilloscope.

Throughout this module we use what we call *notional firing rates* to indicate the relative levels of activity of cells under various stimulus conditions. For simplicity, we have made these rates simply numbers between 0 and 100 and ascribed them no units of measurement. They are meant to index the direction and, very approximately, the magnitude of changes in neuronal activity. In general, a notional firing rate of 100 indicates that the cell is firing very rapidly, usually in response to very intense stimulation. A firing rate of 0 indicates that the cell is not firing at all, which suggests some kind of inhibition of its activity, because even with no external stimulation (no environmental input) a certain amount of spontaneous cell firing occurs. We usually index this background or baseline activity with a notional firing rate around 25. In actuality, neurons with small fibers may fire at rates up to 800 times a second under very intense stimulation, although this will vary with the size of the nerve fiber and several other factors. This upper limit on firing is due to the *refractoriness* of neurons; they take a little time to recover after each action potential. Refractoriness is dealt with in detail in Unit 1.3.

Unit 1.2 Action Potentials and Their Conduction

1.2.1 From Resting Potential to Action Potential
1.2.2 Action Potentials
1.2.3 Phases of the Action Potential
1.2.4 Propagation of Action Potentials
1.2.5 Saltatory Conduction
1.2.6 Speed of Axonal Conduction

All living cells have a membrane potential—that is, a difference in electrical potential (or voltage) between the inside and the outside of the cell. Resting membrane potential is the voltage across the cell membrane when the neuron is at rest—that is, when an action potential is not occurring. This resting potential is approximately –70 mV. The sign of this charge is conventionally minus because the inside of the resting cell is negatively charged relative to the exterior.

The charge difference across the cell membrane detectable when the cell is at rest is due to unequal distribution of electrically charged particles (or ions) inside and outside the cell. Four classes of ions are involved in this process: sodium (Na^+), potassium (K^+) and chloride (Cl^-) ions, and intracellular protein molecules called anions (usually designated A^-).

At rest, potassium ions are very concentrated inside the cell, at about 30 times their extracellular concentration, and sodium and chloride ions are very concentrated outside the cell. At rest, the extracellular concentration of chloride ions, for instance, is about 14 times the intracellular concentration.

If an adequate electrical stimulus is applied to a cell membrane, its resting potential is lost—the process of depolarization—and an action potential will occur. It will only occur if the depolarizing stimulus is above threshold level. During an action potential, the charge across the cell membrane is temporarily reversed. The cell becomes internally positive for a fraction of a millisecond, then returns to rest. This transient depolarization, called an *action potential,* sweeps down the axon of the cell. It is attributable to a sudden increase in the permeability of the membrane to sodium ions. This sweeping, transient depolarization is the physiological correlate of information transmission in the nervous system.

A *relative refractory period* (RRP) begins when the membrane potential begins to return to the resting level, just after the apex of the action potential and continues until the negative afterpotential begins. During the RRP the axon will fire, but only to a much stronger depolarizing stimulus than is normally required to trigger an action potential. The negative afterpotential is a period of heightened excitability during which an action potential can be produced by a stimulus of less strength than normally required. The positive afterpotential is a period of normal excitability at the tail end of the action potential.

The principal aim of this unit is to illustrate how action potentials are generated and propagated along the axon. The resting potential is taken as a starting point and you are able to explore in detail the electrochemical processes that underpin the processes of depolarization and eventual repolarization of the cell as an action potential rises and dissipates at a given site on the cell axon (**Interaction 1.2.1**).

As illustrated in Unit 1.1, intracellular monitoring and recording of action potentials is possible using microelectrodes. Subthreshold depolarizing stimuli trigger graded, or proportional, changes in voltage across the cell membrane, but once threshold depolarization is reached an *all or none* action potential is generated. The cell's response is no longer proportional to the stimulus. Action potentials have the same voltage profile irrespective of the voltage of the triggering stimulus (**Interaction 1.2.2**). Thus, action potentials are *all or none* in the sense that they either occur at the largest size possible (if the depolarizing stimulus is above threshold), or not at all (if the stimulus is below threshold). Once triggered, an action potential will travel to the end of the axon or nerve fiber without any decrease in magnitude.

Although an action potential is essentially a rapid and continuous change in membrane potential over time, it can be thought of as having a number of phases or stages. You might find it useful to know precisely what electrochemical events are occurring in each phase of the action potential. You should find **Interaction 1.2.3** helpful in this regard.

As noted, an action potential is a wave of depolarization sweeping down the axon. Because axons convey messages over long distances, it's vital that signals don't lose their strength as they go. Signal strength is maintained by continually regenerating the action potential along the way. Residual depolarization (a positive charge) spreads along the membrane from the action potential site, where it causes the voltage-gated sodium gates to open, regenerating the action potential in the new location. Ahead of the action potential, sodium ions flow into the axon, regenerating and propagating it. In the wake of the action potential, potassium ions rush out of the cell, restoring the negative intracellular (resting) potential.

The last three interactions in this unit are designed to help you understand where and how action potentials are regenerated and precisely how they are transmitted, or conducted, down the axon—particularly in myelinated fibers. Be sure you understand the role that *nodes of Ranvier* play in the conduction process. The rather lighthearted **Interaction 1.2.6** is intended to reinforce a very simple, but important, message: signals are conducted much more rapidly in myelinated than in unmyelinated fibers.

Unit 1.3 Neural Summation, Refractoriness, and Inhibition

1.3.1 Temporal Summation of EPSPs
1.3.2 Spatial Summation of EPSPs
1.3.3 Nerve Impulses and Coding Stimulus Strength
1.3.4 Excitation and Inhibition
1.3.5 EPSPs, IPSPs, and Action Potentials
1.3.6 Absolute and Relative Refractoriness

You will come across frequent references to *presynaptic* and *postsynaptic* neurons. The terms are relational. Because of the chain- or net-like structure of the nervous system, cells are usually both presynaptic in respect of "downstream" cells and postsynaptic in respect of "upstream" cells. In this sense, a cell is typically postsynaptic to the adjacent cell firing immediately before it—signaling to it—and presynaptic with respect to the next cell in the chain or neural network, to which it signals in its turn. You can think of the presynaptic cell as the *sending* cell and the postsynaptic neuron as the *receiving* cell. The receiving cell will typically signal the next cell in the neural network. The presynaptic cell releases neurotransmitter substances, which cross the synaptic cleft and lodge on the membrane of the postsynaptic cell, triggering changes in postsynaptic electrical potential.

It takes about half a millisecond from the time an excitatory nerve impulse reaches the presynaptic membrane until an electrical response can be recorded in the postsynaptic membrane. A millisecond is one-thousandth of a second. This electrical response, called an *excitatory postsynaptic potential*, or EPSP, lasts about 15 milliseconds and diminishes in strength over time.

This postsynaptic electrical response enhances the excitability of the postsynaptic neuron to other stimuli, hence the term EPSP. If this partial depolarization of the postsynaptic membrane exceeds threshold depolarization, an action potential will be generated. Although somewhat variable, the average firing threshold for (say) an anterior motor neuron in the spinal cord is about 11mV above the resting potential of –70mV.

The amount of neurotransmitter released by the presynaptic neuron directly influences the size of the EPSP. In this way, an EPSP is a *graded* potential, in contrast to an action potential, which is *all or none*. A critical feature of these presynaptic depolarizations is that they *summate*, or add together, influencing the postsynaptic potential.

EPSPs coming close together in time, with one arising before the other has fully decayed, can summate; this is the phenomenon of *temporal summation* (see **Interaction 1.3.1**). Activity simultaneously present in a number of adjacent terminal buttons can add together; this is the process of *spatial summation*. You can examine this phenomenon in **Interaction 1.3.2**.

There is a second kind of postsynaptic electrical activity called *inhibitory postsynaptic potentials* (IPSPs), which yields a hyperpolarization of the postsynaptic membrane and decreased excitability. It is important to note that there is spatial and temporal summation of IPSPs as well as EPSPs. So there is a constant interplay of excitatory and inhibitory influences on postsynaptic membranes. Together they determine whether a neuron fires or not. Indeed, it is the simple algebraic sum of the inhibitory and excitatory potentials on the postsynaptic membrane that determines if the postsynaptic neuron will fire. This summation of EPSPs and IPSPs is called *central summation*—a process addressed in **Interaction 1.3.4**.

If threshold depolarization is reached and an action potential is generated, it sweeps both down the axon and back over the *soma*—wiping the slate clean after each nerve impulse and thus facilitating renewed interplay of excitatory and inhibitory influences.

Interaction 1.3.3 introduces the idea of neural coding and, in particular, how the nervous system encodes the attributes or qualities of stimuli impinging upon the sensory receptors. How are the redness and the scent of a rose encoded by the visual and olfactory systems? What property of the electrical signals in the brain signifies the luscious sweetness of a late-picked Riesling, or the bitterness of quinine? We introduce sensory coding in this unit with rather more mundane questions: What is the code for the subjective magnitude of a stimulus? How do neurons signal how much there is of any given stimulus? As you will discover in Interaction 1.3.3, the rate of firing of neurons increases as both stimulus intensity and subjective stimulus intensity, or magnitude, increase.

It appears, then, that rate of firing may be the code for subjective magnitude, but things turn out not to be quite so simple. Other properties of nerve firing appear to be involved in signaling subjective magnitude. Increasing intensity also changes the timing, or temporal patterning, of nerve impulses. At low intensities, firing is quite variable over time, whereas at high intensities it is very regular. It is likely, then, that this temporal patterning also could be a clue to magnitude or intensity.

There is a very brief period after an action potential in which a neuron is wholly incapable of firing again, whatever the magnitude of the stimulus applied. This irrevocably dormant period is called the *absolute refractory period* (ARP). This is followed by a *relative refractory period* (RRP), which begins as the chemical distribution across the cell membrane begins to return to normal (resting potential). During this RRP—which begins just after the apex of the action potential and continues until the negative afterpotential begins—the axon will fire, but only to a much stronger depolarizing stimulus than is normally required to trigger an action potential. **Interaction 1.3.6** is designed to illustrate these principles of absolute and relative refractoriness. The critical point to note is that although increases in a depolarizing stimulus can cause the cell to fire during the RRP, such increases have no effect during the ARP.

The negative afterpotential is a period of heightened excitability during which an action potential can be produced by a stimulus of less strength than normally required. The positive afterpotential is a period of normal excitability at the tail end of the action potential.

Unit 1.4 Information Transmission and the Synapse

1.4.1 Synaptic Transmission
1.4.2 Stages of Neurotransmission
1.4.3 Lock-and-Key Neurotransmitter Action
1.4.4 Classes of Neurotransmitters
1.4.5 Neurotoxin and Drug Effects
1.4.6 Neuromodulators and Response Duration

Neurons do not operate in isolation. They operate as part of a vast constellation, or network, of functionally integrated neurons. It is important to understand how neurons communicate with each other and the conditions under which this communication is enhanced or thwarted. Unit 1.4 is designed to introduce you to some of these key issues.

Neurons typically do not communicate via direct, physical, electrical links; rather, chemical messages are sent from cell to cell across the spaces between them. The junction between two neurons, their point of communication, is called a *synapse*. There is usually an exceedingly tiny gap between neurons—between the terminal button of one neuron and the dendritic processes or cell body (soma) of another—called the *synaptic cleft*. That gap is about 200 angstroms wide. An angstrom unit is a mere hundred-millionth of a centimeter.

If communication between neurons is to be achieved (that is, if electrochemical signals in the nervous system are to reach their destinations), then they must traverse these gaps between neurons. This transmission process, which only occurs in one direction across the synapse, is as fascinating as it is elegant. **Interaction 1.4.1** should help you understand the main principles involved.

I should note in passing, here, that neurons do occasionally communicate via direct links and so-called *electrotonic spread*—sometimes referred to as "decremental conduction" because the charge diminishes with distance along the neuron. But this process is much less important than synaptic transmission.

As noted, synapses relate an axon to either the dendrites of the next cell (*axo-dendritic synapses*), or its soma (*axo-somatic synapses*). *Axo-axonic* synapses can also occur. There are about ten billion synapses in the human brain, each with up to 100 inputs converging on it. As you will see in **Interactions 1.4.1** and **1.4.2**, synaptic transmission is principally a chemical rather than an electrical event. Presynaptic terminals affect postsynaptic membrane potential by means of transmitter substances, or chemical messengers, stored in *synaptic vesicles* until their release, which is triggered by electrical excitation. In the animation in Interaction 1.4.2, we have shown positive sodium ions flowing into the synaptic cleft on each animation cycle (for convenience); in actuality, they are always present in the synaptic cleft. **Interaction 1.4.4** identifies some of the approximately 100 substances that can act as neurotransmitters. This triggering electrical stimulation can be in the form of experimentally induced depolarization, electrotonic conduction in the neuron, or the arrival of an action potential.

Released transmitter substances, or neurotransmitters, diffuse across the synaptic cleft to the postsynaptic membrane, where—if they lodge on and bind to an appropriate receptor site—they can produce an increase in membrane permeability to Na^+ ions. This can result in partial depolarization—sodium ions entering the cell cause the potential across the membrane to drop—and an excitatory postsynaptic potential (EPSP) occurs. The binding of chemical messengers to the postsynaptic cell can also cause hyperpolarization, in which case the synapse is inhibitory and an inhibitory postsynaptic potential occurs (IPSP). EPSPs and IPSPs are dealt with in some detail in Unit 1.3 (Interactions 1.3.4 and 1.3.5); you will find it useful to have a clear understanding of these crucial processes.

Neurotransmitter receptor sites typically are single molecules in the membrane of the postsynaptic cell. It is necessary for a transmitter molecule to lodge on and bind to a site, much as a key fits a lock. But the key must also be able to turn in the lock. As you will see in Interaction 1.4.3, certain substances similar in shape to target neurotransmitters can lodge on a receptor site and block them from binding to the membrane. They are a close fit, but not close enough to allow the key to turn in the lock. So, the key concept to take away from this interaction is that molecules similar in shape to a target neurotransmitter can sit on a receptor site and block it, sometimes with important functional and behavioral consequences.

Blocking of this kind can result in many behavioral effects and even be life threatening (see **Interaction 1.4.5**). Indeed, many psychoactive drugs and poisons have their effects by altering synaptic functioning. They can, for instance, block neurotransmitter release, or interfere with their reuptake by presynaptic neurons; occupy neurotransmitter receptor sites, blocking them; or inhibit the breakdown of neurotransmitters prior to recycling. As you will see in Interaction 1.4.5, anything that disrupts synaptic transmission can impact on experience, action, and (ultimately) viability of the organism.

Interaction 1.4.6 illustrates a simple, but important, principle. As you will see, neurons release chemicals called *neuromodulators* as well as neurotransmitters. Many neuromodulators are peptides, or chains of amino acids. By themselves, they have little effect on a neuron; they act mainly to modulate or change the effects of neurotransmitters. For instance, they may conditionally shorten or prolong the effect of a neurotransmitter.

Unit 1.5 Inhibition, Receptive Fields, and Neural Coding

1.5.1 Lateral Inhibition
1.5.2 Lateral Inhibition and Receptive Fields

1.5.3 Simple Neural Circuits
1.5.4 Neural Code for Quality Across the Senses
1.5.5 Neural Code for Quality Within a Sense
1.5.6 Mapping Receptive Fields

Individual cells in the nervous system interact in complex ways. Lateral inhibition—the reduction in activity in one cell or region caused by activity in a neighboring cell or region—is an example of such interaction. In the visual system, for instance, lateral inhibition can act to heighten the contrast at stimulus borders. In **Interaction 1.5.1** you can simulate Hartline's classical demonstration of lateral inhibition in the compound eye of a horseshoe crab.

In the horseshoe crab, or limulus, the lateral plexus is the mechanism for lateral inhibition. This weblike structure allows the activity of one cell to influence the activity of another. The firing rate of one photoreceptor can be progressively reduced, or inhibited, as the activity in a nearby receptor increases. In Interaction 1.5.1, first note the background firing rate when both lights are off. Then switch on light A and continue to monitor the firing rate. Finally, switch on light B. The crucial feature of this interaction is what happens when the brightness of B is progressively increased: lateral inhibition will increase, reducing the firing rate of cell A.

It is clear that lateral inhibition plays an important role in building the receptive fields of neurons in the visual system. In **Interaction 1.5.2**, you can explore how connections in the vertebrate retina accomplish lateral inhibition. The key lies in the role played by widely branching horizontal cells in inhibiting nearby bipolar cells when excited by receptors. For instance, in the highly schematic model of a vertebrate retina shown in Interaction 1.5.2, receptor R3 both excites the bipolar cell (B3) and the red horizontal cell. It is important to note that the excited horizontal cell, in turn, inhibits several nearby bipolar cells, inducing lateral inhibition in them.

In Interaction 1.5.2, B3 is inhibited slightly by the horizontal cell, of course, but it remains positive (check the voltmeter) because it is directly excited by R3. None of the other receptor cells is activated. As you activate receptor cells R4 through R6, in turn, take care to note how the adjacent cells are laterally inhibited via the horizontal cell. Again, the critical point in this interaction is that the horizontal cell, stimulated by the active receptor, is in a state of net excitation, inhibiting all nearby bipolar cells. The bipolar cell directly excited by the receptor firing also remains in a state of net excitation—but all other bipolar cells are inhibited.

The nervous system not only passively conducts neural signals over relatively long distances, it processes them in subtle and powerful ways, principally by convergence and inhibition at the synapses. It does this by forming networks of nerve fibers, so-called *neural networks*. As messages travel through these vast networks, they are continuously shaped, analyzed, and transformed in ways that allow information to be transmitted and assimilated more efficiently. Neurons progressively become specialized to respond optimally to a particular pattern of stimulation. As previously alluded to, two processes play pivotal roles: convergence and inhibition.

Convergence occurs when two or more neurons synapse onto a third neuron. In this way, cells may collect and integrate information from many other cells. These connections may be *excitatory*, in which case activity in the target cell will tend to increase, or *inhibitory*, causing target cell activity to decrease. Together, convergence and inhibition can have powerful logical consequences. You can explore three simple neural circuits in **Interaction 1.5.3**, for example. The first—a simple linear circuit—exhibits neither convergence nor inhibition; the second involves convergence alone; and the third entails both convergence and inhibition. The important thing to monitor in this interaction is the firing rate of neuron I. It fires in response to different properties of the input from the receptors in each case.

A linear circuit is one in which all the synapses are excitatory and the signal generated by each receptor travels directly to the next neuron with no other neurons involved. As lights are added in Interaction 1.5.3, we are effectively turning the spot of light into a bar of light of increasing length. Note that the number of neurons firing increases linearly with bar length. The firing rate of cell I does not change, irrespective of how many receptor neurons are stimulated.

In the second class of neural circuit discussed in this interaction, all the synapses are excitatory, but convergence is now incorporated. Convergence occurs when two or more neurons synapse on a single neuron, so receptors A and B converge on neuron H; F and G converge on J; and so on. So, cells collect information from other cells. I's firing rate will increase linearly with the number of receptors stimulated, and we can monitor the output of the entire circuit by monitoring a single neuron, rather than counting the number of neurons firing. Because of this property of convergence, the firing rate of I signals information about the population of receptors as a whole.

The final class of circuit in Interaction 1.5.3 incorporates *both* the processes of inhibition and convergence. It is important to note that two inhibitory synapses are included in this final circuit. H and J inhibit neuron I. So, this circuit responds best to (fires maximally to) a bar of light whose length is such that it illuminates only receptors C, D, and E. If the bar of light extends to stimulate A and B or F and G, the firing rate will fall way because their input to I is inhibitory as well.

The key point to take away from this interaction is that the neurons in these latter two classes of circuits not only transmit information, but they process it by means of convergence and inhibition.

All sensory signals have similar properties. Simply monitoring a cell's activity can provide no clues as to whether it represents an auditory, olfactory, or somaesthetic signal. **Interaction 1.5.4** raises the question as to how sensory modality is represented in the nervous system. The message to take away from this simple interaction is that, because each sensory signal travels in specific nervous pathways and finishes up at a particular location on the cortex, its modality is implicitly coded by its path and destination. Thus, a message that reaches the auditory cortex via the auditory nerve necessarily represents a sound.

This begs the question as to how sensory attributes are encoded or represented by the nervous system *within a sensory* modality—an issue explored in **Interaction 1.5.5**. How are the intramodality qualities of (say) sweetness, bitterness, and saltiness encoded? The challenge, here, is to identify the information contained in the nerve impulses that uniquely signals the presence of these different properties in a stimulus. One key distinction that you should understand in detail is that between so-called *labeled-lines* and *across-fiber pattern coding* of stimulus attributes. You will encounter it often, particularly in Unit 1.8.

At one extreme, properties like "sweetness," "pungency," "acidity," "hue," and so on, could be signaled by activity in a specific nerve fiber, or line. Activity in fiber A, for instance, could denote that the property of "saltiness" was present. You might think of that line as being *labeled* "salty." This is the essence of *specificity theory.*

But specificity theory has problems: there are simply too many identifiable stimulus qualities (colors, forms, smells, and tastes) to be explained in terms of a neuron that fires only to one specific perceptual quality. Moreover, there is little evidence that these kinds of highly specific neurons actually exist in the nervous system. Similarly, tuned cells tend also to respond to stimulus intensity, so that a given rate of firing cannot unambiguously signal a given simple attribute.

An alternative to labeled lines coding is across-fiber pattern coding, which is dealt with in more detail in Unit 1.8. In essence, it suggests that sensory qualities are signaled to the brain by the pattern of activity across a large number of neurons, rather than one. Qualities are differentiated by the overall pattern of firing across many neurons—their global response profile.

In the human retina, more than 126 million receptors converge onto about 1 million retinal ganglion cells. So each ganglion cell receives input from, or is stimulated by, many retinal cells, about 126 on average. Those ganglion cells also receive inhibitory input from horizontal and amacrine cells.

It is possible to map the receptive field of a retinal ganglion cell (usually in a cat or monkey) by monitoring the firing of the target cell with an intracellular microelectrode. Typically, stimuli are projected onto a screen in front of the animal whose eye is kept stationary. This is equivalent to shining the stimulus on a particular area of the retina: each point on the screen corresponds to a point on the retina. As the stimulus is translated across the screen, the cell's activity is recorded. If an excitatory response (that is, an increase in the cell's firing rate) is observed, that point is marked with a "+." If stimulation in a particular region reduces, or inhibits, the firing rate, that point is marked with a "–."

Typically, these pluses and minuses define concentric regions, one circle inside another, together known as a *center-surround receptive field.* Some fields have the pluses in the middle, surrounded by minuses. These are called excitatory-center–inhibitory-surround receptive fields (or, sometimes ON-center–OFF-surround fields). Others have the minuses in the central region surrounded by a region of pluses. Not surprisingly, these are called inhibitory-center–excitatory-surround receptive fields (or, sometimes, OFF-center–ON-surround fields).

Interaction 1.5.6 simulates an experiment in which a receptive field is mapped. A point of light is translated back and forth (in practice, point by point) across a dark screen—and, in turn, the retina—while the cell's firing rate is monitored. If the firing rate goes up, a plus is recorded in that spot. If it goes down, a minus is recorded. This continues until the whole receptive field of the hypothetical ganglion cell is mapped. The key point to grasp here is the logic of receptive field mapping.

Unit 1.6 Receptive Fields

1.6.1 Stimulus Size and Receptive Fields
1.6.2 Grating-Phase and Ganglion Cell Responses
1.6.3 Receptive Fields and Stimulus Size and Shape
1.6.4 Simple Cells in the Cortex
1.6.5 Complex Cells in the Cortex
1.6.6 Hypercomplex Cells in the Cortex

The concept of receptive fields, introduced in Unit 1.5, is extended in Unit 1.6 to include the more complex receptive fields of cells in the striate cortex. All of the interactions in this unit allow you to monitor the notional firing rates of cells under varying stimulus conditions. They are all based on the ground-breaking work of David Hubel and Torsten Wiesel, who shared the 1981 Nobel prize in physiology and medicine for their contribution to our understanding of the human visual system. Interactions 1.6.1 to 1.6.3 all deal with the center-surround receptive fields of retinal ganglion cells, so-called because the center and the surround regions of the field cause the cell to behave in different ways.

The firing rate of a cell with an ON-center (or excitatory-center) receptive field will increase if its center region alone is stimulated (say) with a tiny spot of light. ON-center receptive fields typically have OFF surrounds (that is, inhibitory surrounds). Thus, if the periphery alone of this kind of receptive field is stimulated, the firing rate of the ganglion cell will diminish from its baseline rate and may cease entirely. This situation is reversed in the case of cells with OFF-center receptive fields. Stimulation of the center alone is inhibitory. Stimulation of the surround alone is excitatory. Outside the laboratory, it is more likely, of course, that parts of both the center and surround of a given receptive field will be stimulated, yielding a firing rate that is intermediate. This is because the center and surround are antagonistic; inhibitory and excitatory influences will be summed.

In **Interaction 1.6.1**, you have the opportunity to increase the size of a spot of light falling on center-surround receptive fields, both ON-center and OFF-center. Monitor the notional firing rate of the cell carefully as the region stimulated by the spot of light varies. You will note that the optimal stimulus for an ON-center field—that which maximizes the firing rate of the ganglion cell—is a spot of light that covers the center of the field, but does not impinge on the inhibitory surround. Although this condition is not simulated in the interaction, it should be clear to you that the optimal stimulus for an OFF-center field is an annulus of light that covers the surround of the field, but does not impinge on its inhibitory center.

Analogous work has been done using as stimuli gratings of light and dark bars of varying spatial frequency and spatial phase (see Unit 4.7 for explorations of the properties of gratings). Some of these conditions are simulated in **Interaction 1.6.2** and you are able to monitor the activity of a retinal ganglion cell as the spatial relationship between the receptive field and the grating is varied. It is vital that you understand why the activity of the ganglion cell changes as it does.

A critical feature of receptive fields is that they vary in *size* and, accordingly, activity will vary across cells in response to a grating of fixed spatial phase and frequency (**Interaction 1.6.3**). Thus, phase, frequency, field size, and the topographical location of excitatory and inhibitory regions within the field, will jointly determine the ganglion cell response. This is the key message to be gleaned from Interactions 1.6.1 to 1.6.3.

The last three interactions in this unit are designed to give you some understanding of the nature of the receptive fields of three classes of neurons in the striate (and, occasionally, the extrastriate) cortex: simple cortical cells, complex cortical cells, and hypercomplex or end-stopped cells. These are dealt with in Interactions 1.6.4 to 1.6.6, respectively.

You will notice in **Interaction 1.6.4** that the receptive fields of simple cortical cells resemble the retinal ganglion cells' center-surround fields in that they have distinct excitatory and inhibitory regions. But, rather than these areas forming concentric circles, they are configured in bands, side by side. This arrangement has important consequences; it determines that the optimal stimulus for simple cortical cells will be a bar of light oriented along the axis of the excitatory region. Thus, a simple cortical cell will fire maximally when a bar of light lies squarely along the excitatory region. As is clear from this interaction, tilting the bar of light causes it to impinge on and stimulate the adjacent inhibitory regions of the receptive field—thus reducing the firing rate of the cell.

Although the axis of orientation of the field used in Interaction 1.6.4 is vertical, Hubel and Wiesel found evidence for horizontally and diagonally oriented simple cell receptive fields. In summary, then, these simple cells in the striate cortex have a preference for (respond maximally to) light bars with particular orientations. They will, nevertheless respond to simple points or spots of light. Many complex cells also respond optimally to a particular direction of movement.

Interaction 1.6.5 enables you to explore the properties of receptive fields of *complex cortical cells*. It lets you monitor complex cell activity, while varying the orientation and location of a bar of light in the receptive field. What you will find is that a complex cell responds best when an optimally oriented light bar is moved across the entire receptive field in a particular direction. Unlike simple cells, complex cortical cells normally do not respond to stationary bars or spots or points of light.

So-called hypercomplex, or end-stopped, cells are dealt with in **Interaction 1.6.6**. You will discover that these cells respond best to a moving line, or light bar, of specific length moving in a defined direc-

tion in the receptive field. This sensitivity to stimulus length sets hypercomplex cells apart from complex cortical cells, which are indifferent to length. If a stimulus is too long, a hypercomplex cell simply will not fire. As well as being sensitive to light lines or bars, hypercomplex cells also fire to moving light angles or corners.

What emerges from the study of these three classes of cortical cells is the idea that they effectively act as feature detectors. As we progress from retina to cortex, we find that neurons respond to progressively more specific stimuli. There is clearly a good deal of information processing occurring as signals move upstream in the visual system. Moreover, this feature detection and information processing continues beyond the striate cortex.

Unit 1.7 Sensory Receptors

1.7.1 The Structure of the Eye
1.7.2 The Retina and Rod-Cone Distributions
1.7.3 The Structure of the Ear
1.7.4 The Skin and Somaesthesis
1.7.5 The Nose and Olfaction
1.7.6 Taste Buds and Taste

The ease with which the senses are used belies the sophistication and complexity of the processes that underlie sensation and perception. We are immersed in a restless sea of ever-changing physical energies—photic, mechanical, chemical, and thermal—that ebbs and flows relentlessly, driving our sensory experiences and shaping what we know of the world around us. We know the world only through our senses; they are our windows on the world. Without them we would live in a dark, silent, colorless, tasteless, feelingless void; the world would not exist for us.

These physical energies impinge, or stimulate, the brain through specialized receptors tuned to respond to very narrow bands of energy. In this way, sensory systems are sensitive to very little of what is "out there." Moreover, as the senses turn environmental energies into electrical signals representing those energies and their sources, the world is effectively filtered and transformed. In this way, internalized representations of environmental stimuli are highly selective: we hear only those sounds with frequencies between 20 and 20,000 Hz, for instance, and are visually sensitive only to electromagnetic energy with wavelengths between, roughly, 340 and 760 nanometers. Ultrasound is not heard; nor are the infrared and ultraviolet segments of the electromagnetic spectrum normally seen.

It is a classical truism, of course, that the eyes do not see, the ears do not hear, the nose does not smell—they are simply specialized constellations of receptors, part of the system. In this sense, Unit 1.7, focusing on the main sensory receptors, tells only part of the story. The receptors play an important, but limited, role in sensation and perception, that of specialized stimulus transduction and encoding.

It may be useful to note the properties sensory receptors have in common before dealing with the features that make them unique. For example, although receptors are uniquely responsive to a particular kind of energy, they sometimes respond to others. For instance, although the eye is maximally sensitive to certain wavelengths of electromagnetic energy, pressing on the eye can result in a distinctly visual impression. Mechanical energy can cause the neurons in the retina to respond. But, no matter how firing of the visual receptors is effected, the sensory impression is quintessentially *visual.* This notion that a sensation depends on the receptor stimulated, not the mode or manner of its stimulation, is called the *law of specific nerve energies.*

All receptors produce slow, graded, local generator potentials. The magnitude of these generator potentials reflects the intensity or strength of the stimulus and, in turn, the number of action potentials that occur. Not only do sensory receptors respond to stimuli in a graded, rather than all-or-none, fashion, they are also uniquely sensitive to changing—rather than steady state—stimulation. Firing rates typically fall away under conditions of constant stimulation. Receptors seem uniquely tuned to monitor for survival-threatening change in environmental stimuli.

All of the interactions in this unit have both a learning/exploration phase and a testing phase. They are all designed to achieve much the same end: to leave you with a mastery of at least the broad structure and function of the sensory systems. The aim is to deal with the respective systems in the kind of detail likely to be useful to an advanced undergraduate sensation and perception student. Although reasonably comprehensive, the list of structures identified is far from exhaustive.

Note that **Interactions 1.7.1** and **1.7.2** are both devoted to the eye. The first deals with the structure and function of the eye *in globo,* whereas the second provides an opportunity to explore the detail of the retina. This emphasis is justified by the importance of the visual system in human functioning and the fact that we know a good deal more about it than the other sensory systems. The gustatory, olfactory, and somaesthetic systems, for instance, are poorly understood by comparison.

Pay special attention to the opportunity to map rod and cone densities on the retina in Interaction 1.7.2. Differences in the spatial distribution of rods and cones across the retina have important functional consequences for human vision: the preponderance of cones in the fovea means excellent fine-grained discrimination in that region, whereas acuity diminishes rapidly towards the periphery, where rods predominate; the absence of photoreceptors where the ganglion cell fibers bundle and exit the eye leaves the eye effectively blind in that region; and foveal night vision is very poor because of its concentration of primarily photopic cones.

This unit concentrates on the basic structure and function of the sense organs, but you will find many other related interactions sprinkled throughout the package. For instance, there are interactions exploring aspects of retinal function such as lateral inhibition (Interaction 1.5.1) and ganglion cell receptive fields (Interactions 1.5.6 and 1.6.1. to 1.6.3). Much of the material in the color-vision module (Module 3) will provide insights into the coding of color by retinal photoreceptors and related phenomena. **Interaction 1.7.3**, on the ear, is complemented by interactions such as 1.8.5 and 1.8.6; **Interaction 1.7.5**, dealing with the nose and olfaction, is augmented by material in Interactions 1.8.2 and 1.8.3. I would encourage you to use the Organizer to search for materials related to this unit.

It is worth noting, in conclusion that every sensory modality is subject to distortions, illusions, and systematic errors that misrepresent the environment to our consciousness. There are illusions of taste, touch, olfaction, and audition as well as visual illusions.

Unit 1.8 Neural Coding of Sensory Properties

1.8.1 Labeled-Lines and Across-Fiber Coding
1.8.2 Spatial Coding of Odor Quality
1.8.3 Neural Coding of Odor
1.8.4 Coding Somatosensory Stimuli
1.8.5 Place Model of Pitch Perception
1.8.6 Volley Model of Pitch Perception

The ability to monitor and analyze electrical activity in the brain has long held out the beguiling promise that we might some day be able to reduce what we know of sensation, perception, memory, and cognition, for instance, to the explanatory principles of neurophysiology. To date, progress has been modest. We presently are able to draw little more than loose parallels between patterns of cerebral activity and aspects of sensation and perception. Part of the problem is that we don't know that what we are able to record is actually used by the brain. Although we can identify patterns of information in neural signals, we don't know how (or even if) they are utilized. Much of what we have been able to observe may be irrelevant, or germane in ways that we cannot presently discern. Nowhere are these problems more clearly evident than in the neural coding of sensory qualities.

We know the world only indirectly, after it has been selectively filtered, transformed, and encoded by the receptors and after it has been further processed by the higher centers and pathways of the brain. Thus, perception is based on very indirect representations indeed. Clearly, properties of the external world are encoded electrochemically, but this begs the question as to how properties of the world are represented in that sensory code. How do electrical signals in the nervous system represent properties of the environment? This is the problem of sensory coding. We encounter it again and again: How is red represented? How is a high pitch coded? How is coldness or pain encoded in the complex signals echoing in the brain? Indeed, how does the brain distinguish between sights and smells and sounds?

In his *doctrine of specific nerve energies,* Müller (1842) suggested that the brain receives information by means of signals in sensory nerves and that it distinguishes between senses by monitoring the activity of particular nerves. Thus, for Müller, activity in the optic nerve signaled light, for instance, whereas activity in the auditory nerve signaled sound. It was soon found, however, that each of these nerves projects to a particular area of the cortex, and the principle was amended to suggest that the sense that is stimulated is signaled by the location at which the electrical signal reaches the brain.

A more interesting question, perhaps, concerns how we code for particular stimulus qualities with a given sense modality. For instance, what information is encoded in the signal that denotes "red," or "salt," or "yellow," or "sweet," or "acrid"?

The context in which neurons exist—with the constellation of excitatory and inhibitory exerted on them—means that they tend to respond best to certain stimuli and their firing can signal the presence of a particular environmental attribute. Thus, the responses of specifically tuned neurons can provide the sensory code. This is the central notion of *specificity theory.*

In essence, specificity theory posits that there are specifically tuned neurons, which provide information about specific qualities of the environment. This tuning of a neuron to a specific optimal stimulus is accomplished by the neural processes of convergence, excitation, and inhibition acting in concert. In addition, neurons are tuned by receiving input from receptors tuned to respond only to a specific stimulus. Specificity theory is equated in this unit with *labeled-lines coding.* But specificity theory has problems. For instance, there are simply too many identifiable stimulus qualities (colors, forms, smells, and tastes) to be explained in terms of neurons that fire only to one specific perceptual quality. Moreover, there is little evidence that these kinds of highly specific neurons actually exist in the nervous system. Similarly, tuned cells tend also to respond to stimulus intensity, so that a given rate of firing cannot unambiguously signal a given simple attribute.

It is clear, then, that specificity theory, in and of itself, is not the answer to the problem of sensory coding, although it appears to play some role. In this unit, specificity theory is contrasted with *across-fiber pattern theory,* in which sensory qualities are signaled to the brain by the pattern of activity across a large number of neurons. Qualities are differentiated by the overall pattern of firing across many neurons—the global response profile. In this sense, each attribute, or quality, has a distinctive "signature" of activity in a constellation of cells.

Thus, it is possible to distinguish labeled-lines coding from across-fiber coding of sensory quality, and that distinction—an important one—is encountered several times throughout this unit. **Interaction 1.8.1** contrasts the two coding systems using the analogy of a waiter signaling a cook in the kitchen. The key point to take away from this interaction is that across-fiber coding is much more powerful. Given three functional lights (the equivalent of neurons) labeled-lines coding enables the waiter to signal only three different dishes. If across-fiber coding is substituted—and one dish is signaled by each of the possible *combinations*, or *patterns*, of light—one can signal seven dishes, rather than three (assuming all three lights off is considered a null signal).

As you will learn in **Interaction 1.8.2**, the olfactory bulb is a complicated brain nucleus on which the axons of olfactory receptor cells converge and terminate. It appears that odor quality may be coded by the spatial pattern of neural activity across the olfactory bulb. This is a nice example of across-fiber pattern coding. The key point is that because each olfactory receptor cell responds to several odors, odor can't be coded by the activity of a single cell in isolation; labeled-lines coding simply could not work under these conditions. A given cell enters into the spatial patterns indicative of several odors.

There is some evidence that a more accurate description of the odor detection system lies in a *hybrid* system, incorporating elements of both labeled-lines and across-fiber coding. In **Interaction 1.8.3** we look at one such hybrid model, based primarily on labeled-lines coding but using across-fiber comparison to resolve ambiguity. It is built on the idea that each olfactory receptor has a preferred odor to which it responds most strongly, but it also responds to other related and unrelated molecules. In this way, the activity of any given receptor will be highly indicative of the stimulus odor but, ultimately, ambiguous—not least because odor concentrations will vary. Thus, the most active receptor ambiguously signals which molecules could be present, and across-fiber comparison of activity in the stimulated receptors resolves that ambiguity. The important point is that it is not always the most active receptor that signals the actual odor present.

The cutaneous sensory system, which you can explore in **Interaction 1.8.4**, is one of the most interesting, but least understood, of the sensory systems. You will see that it appears to have a strong labeled-lines coding component: specific receptors appear to signal specific kinds of stimulation. But, paradoxically, many receptors appear to signal more than one class of sensory attribute or quality. Across-fiber coding is almost certainly implicated, but we currently know little of the detail of how this is achieved.

This unit concludes with two models of pitch perception in the auditory system which, by contrast, is relatively well understood. Pitch coding appears to be another hybrid system, with facets of both types of coding. According to the *volley principle* (**Interaction 1.8.6**), not all nerve fibers fire at the same time. Rather, a volley of cell firings is staggered or distributed in time. Taken as a whole, their collective activity reflects the frequency of the stimulus. Each hair cell responds to some of the sound waves only. Combined, the cells' activity accurately reflects the frequency of the stimulus. Summed over time, the cell's activity resembles a volley.

Module 2

Form, Pattern, and Movement

Unit 2.1 Gestalt Laws of Organization

2.1.1 The Law of Proximity
2.1.2 The Law of Similarity
2.1.3 The Law of Simplicity or Good Figure
2.1.4 The Law of Common Fate
2.1.5 The Law of Good Continuation
2.1.6 The Law of Closure

Knowledge of the explanatory principles of Gestalt psychology—in particular, the Gestalt laws of perceptual organization or grouping—will come in very handy as you work through the units in this module. As you will see in later units, the early Gestaltists—Kurt Koffka, Wolfgang Köhler, and Max Wertheimer principal among them—were very much concerned with the perception of form or figure. Not least, with how we select, organize, and group elements in the visual field to constitute those perceptual wholes we see as figures or objects. They formulated a set of rules outlining the bases on which elements combine to form integrated perceptual wholes. These Gestalt *laws of organization* allow one to predict what will be perceived, given certain stimulus conditions—at least in an interesting, if somewhat limited, variety of situations.

The Gestaltists argued that when elements or features are organized into figures or forms, those wholes are different in essential ways from the component parts. For instance, we tend to group elements that are relatively closer to each other than to other elements in the field (**Interaction 2.1.1**). This is known as the *law of proximity*: things in close proximity to one another seem to belong together, for reasons that are relatively poorly understood. This is most often true when those elements are undifferentiated or, in a sense, meaningless. Where categorical differences exist between elements in the field of view, they may be spontaneously grouped on the basis of their conceptual or physical similarity—even when those elements are equally spaced (**Interaction 2.1.2**). This clearly implies a degree of classification or recognition prior to grouping.

It is possible, clearly, to pit similarity and proximity qua grouping principles, or tendencies, against each other. Although there are conditions under which one can group according to either principle, there appears always to be an extreme condition where grouping is wholly determined. For instance, if the columns of a matrix of elements are sufficiently separated laterally, the heterogeneous elements within them will be grouped, even though the possibility exists that those elements could be seen as homogeneous rows.

So, when more than one option is available, there often is a degree of conscious choice, or volition, as to which grouping principle is adopted—at least within certain defined limits. It seems to be impossible, however, to "see" a stimulus grouped on two conflicting principles simultaneously. If you group by similarity, you cannot simultaneously group by proximity.

At the heart of this approach is the idea that perception cannot be broken down into elementary sense components; the perceptual whole is different from its parts and cannot be decomposed without losing its essential quality. The whole, the form, the figure or *Gestalt* is the fundamental unit of perception. In the same sense that something is irretrievably lost when a melody is broken down into its constituent notes, so a visual form cannot be decomposed into its elements without loss. The essence of the melody is in the context and relationships between the parts—in their configuration, the *Gestalt*.

This brings us to an important point: just as proximity can be *spatial* it can also be *temporal*. Events (sounds, for instance) relatively close together in *time* will tend to be grouped. So will *similar* notes or tones. It is not difficult to imagine, then, the important role Gestalt grouping principles play in music. We see this same parallel at work in the third of the laws of organization: the *law of good configuration*, sometimes known as the *law of Pragnänz*, the *law of simplicity*, or the *law of good figure*.

The *law of Pragnänz* is rather more abstract than the Gestalt principles discussed so far. It is the tendency to see things as belonging together if they form a *good* figure. If you think this begs the question as to what is a *good* figure, you are quite right. A great deal of time and effort has gone into trying to define what makes a figure *good*. In general terms, the law of Pragnänz—the pivotal principle of Gestalt grouping—

suggests that stimulus patterns are perceived such that the resulting structure is as simple as possible. There appears to be a tendency to group discrete elements that appear to follow a smooth curve; a straight line; or a regular, repetitive pattern. They have the property of continuity. This is an example of *good continuation* (for other examples see **Interaction 2.1.5**).

Figural simplicity is an important consideration in grouping and form perception. We tend to resolve and perceive stimuli with multiple possible resolutions, or interpretations, in the simplest possible terms. Simplicity is not itself a simple concept! One way of expressing this property is in information theory terms, by equating it with minimum-information configurations. Information has a strict mathematical description, and information content, expressed in *bits*, is a useful metric. You can explore information theory in detail in Unit 5.4.

In this sense, the simplest figure is that which can be specified in terms of the minimum number of bits of information. A figure that is a member of a class that contains only eight equipossible members can be specified by three bits of information. In these terms, the more predictable a figure, the lower its information content, the simpler it is. Simple, predictable figures are said to possess good form.

There is another principle of Pragnänz related to continuity: the *law of closure*. We have a tendency to see figures as whole, or complete, bounded entities—even when they are not! **Interaction 2.1.6** provides examples of such forms where the contours are broken or incomplete. Even so, we tend to perceive those figures in their archetypal, quintessential, complete forms.

We tend to see complex objects as comprising parts that naturally cohere, or have an ineluctable unity. **Interaction 2.1.3** gives you three examples. You will tend to see them as being "built" from certain elements—the *good continuation* resolution or analysis—and yet alternative constructions, or interpretations, are equally possible. You might find it interesting to try to generate analogous figures yourself.

Interaction 2.1.4 is a compelling example of the *law of common fate*: elements moving in the same direction tend to be grouped. You also can think of this example as a special case of the *law of similarity*, where elements with a similar direction of movement are grouped. This raises an interesting issue: similarity per se embraces a vast variety of attributes, in isolation and in combination. Elements can be similar in hue, size, lightness, shape, pitch, length—the list is endless.

As noted, several Gestalt grouping principles apply to auditory as well as visual stimuli. The sounds around us can be said to compose an auditory scene. Just as visual stimuli are perceptually organized according to Gestalt principles, so sounds or tones in the auditory scene are perceived as belonging together. Thus, similar tones—those with similar pitch, for instance—are grouped perceptually, as are tones relatively close together in time. These two grouping principles are not independent. Tones similar in pitch, but too far apart in time, will not be grouped. There is also evidence for the law of good continuation operating the auditory domain (Warren, Obuseck, & Acroff, 1972).

Another important Gestalt grouping principle is the *law of meaningfulness*, sometimes called the law of *familiarity*: elements are more likely to be grouped if they jointly constitute, or define, a meaningful, familiar form. There is a powerful incidental demonstration of this principle at work in Interaction 2.3.6.

Together, the Gestalt principles, or grouping tendencies, explored in this unit appear to contribute to the speed and stability of human perception. They can also lead to measurable distortions or misperceptions. For instance, when elements are grouped on the basis of the Gestalt principles of similarity, proximity, closure, and good continuation, that grouping causes measurable distortions in the perceived distance between elements, that is, their spatial distribution (Coren & Girgus, 1980; Enns & Girgus, 1985). In general, elements grouped together are perceived as being closer together than nongrouped equidistant elements. Interestingly, these spatial distortions tend to decrease with age (Enns & Girgus, 1985).

Unit 2.2 Figure and Ground

Object (or form) perception seems to be a relatively simple process that usually can be achieved without much cognitive effort. This apparent simplicity is deceptive. When researchers have attempted to program computers to accomplish elementary object recognition they have found it a very thorny problem indeed. Even after decades of research, computers still have great difficulty reliably recognizing everyday objects.

Object recognition requires, as a first step, segregation of an object (or figure) from the background against which it is viewed (ground).

This unit provides several explorations, which I hope will help you understand the processes involved in so-called *figure-ground segregation,* a precondition of object recognition. There is evidence that figure-ground segregation is a very basic process, and that this ability is independent of learning. People unable to see until adulthood differentiate figure from ground immediately after their sight is restored (von Senden, 1960), even when they cannot discriminate and recognize forms or objects.

Figure, in this context, refers to the central object attended to in a scene, and *ground* refers to the remainder of the scene after the figure has been segregated. Part of the analytical problem is that a certain part in any differentiated field—the figure—appears to stand out "quite naturally" from the ground.

Danish psychologist Edgar Rubin was one of the first to try to formulate general principles governing figure-ground segregation: "The following principle is fundamental: if one of the two homogeneous, different-colored fields is larger than and encloses the other, there is a great likelihood that the small, surrounded field will be seen as figure" (Rubin 1915/1958, p. 202). This unit illustrates a number of other key variables that appear to be involved, including symmetry, relative size or area, convexity-concavity, orientation, spatial frequency, and meaning. Thus (in very general terms) symmetrical, smaller, convex, horizontally and vertically oriented, high-spatial frequency, and meaningful forms tend to be seen as "figure." As you will see, the deceptively simple segregation of figure from ground is, in fact, a complex matter.

It is not always the case, for instance, that one region always encloses another. The parts of a field may share a common contour, so that there is no necessary tendency for either to be seen as figure. In this case, figure-ground ambiguity is said to exist. The region seen as figure may flip to be seen as ground, and vice versa. It is relatively easy to switch at will between figure and ground in ambiguous figures. Happily, figure-ground ambiguity seldom occurs in the world of natural objects. Still, an interesting real-world example is given in **Interaction 2.2.2**: the vase shown was manufactured by Kaiser Porcelain Limited as a wedding anniversary gift for Queen Elizabeth II and the Duke of Edinburgh. Their profiles are incorporated in its outline shape.

Rubin defined figure as having the quality of a "thing" and ground as having the quality of a "substance." This old distinction bears consideration. Whereas the figure appears to possess the defining edge separating figure from ground—and appears more dominant, memorable, and impressive—the ground typically appears shapeless or formless and recessive. By definition, the figure will appear closer to the viewer than the ground, which appears to extend behind the figure. This entails that when figure and ground are resolved, the scene takes on a quality of depth or three-dimensionality not present to that point.

It is all-but impossible simultaneously to see a region as both figure and ground, that is, to see (say) both the faces and the vase in the Rubin vase.

A surprising aspect of the figure-ground distinction is that a region of constant lightness appears lighter when perceived as figure than when seen as ground. Similarly, a region seen as figure shows greater simultaneous lightness contrast (is affected more by its contrast with the surrounding ground) than does the same region seen as ground. This phenomenon is known as the Wolff effect.

Bev Doolittle's pintos in **Interaction 2.2.1** not only provide an interesting study in figure-ground segregation, they also illustrate some of the Gestalt laws of grouping (see Unit 2.1) in action. Indeed, they show how the latter can assist in achieving the former. By grouping areas of similar shading in the horses' legs and bodies (the law of similarity) and isolating the smooth contours of their back and legs (the law of good continuation), we are better able to separate figure from ground (Goldstein, 1996, pp. 186–187).

Interactions 2.2.2 to 2.2.6 illustrate the roles of area, symmetry, spatial frequency, and meaning in determining the region of a figure that will be seen as figure. In general, the smaller of two regions will be seen as figure, and symmetrical forms will tend to be seen as figure with unsymmetrical regions seen as ground. Where regions are defined by patterns or gratings, those with high-spatial frequencies will usually be seen as figure and those with low-spatial frequencies as ground. **Interaction 2.2.6** gives a dramatic illustration of the role meaning can play in determining figure-ground segregation. Initially, the meaningless black forms are seen as figure on a light beige ground. As soon as meaning emerges, figure and ground are reversed. As you work through them, try to assimilate and state the general principles of figure-ground segregation at work in these interactions and to develop your own examples as you go.

You may find it interesting, also, to relate the figure-ground interactions in this unit to those on subjective, or illusory, contours in Unit 2.3. Subjective contours usually define illusory figures, which have the same quality of anomalous lightness as conventional figures: regions defined as figure appear lighter than the physically identical grounds "against" which they are seen. In essence, there is a change of lightness at an illusory contour, even though that contour is not physically present.

Unit 2.3 Illusory Contours

A cornerstone of Gestalt psychology has been the notion that the perceptual whole is somehow more than—or, at least, different from—the sum of its parts. Gestaltists have argued that there appear to be so-called emergent properties of perceptual objects, which are not readily explicable in terms of the constituent parts from which they derive. Apparent movement is a good case in point. If we rapidly alternate two frames, or pictures, in which an object in frame 1 is slightly displaced in frame 2, that object will appear to oscillate back and forth in the space between the two locations. You will find several examples of this way of generating apparent movement in Units 2.5 to 2.7.

Gestaltists would argue that this apparent movement is an emergent property. The perceived stimulus is not only moving, when the frames are merely still pictures, but it is seen in the space between its locations in the two frames—where no stimulus object physically exists.

A second class of apparently emergent phenomena is presently attracting a good deal of research interest, so-called *subjective, apparent,* or *illusory contours.* This unit contains several examples. Illusory contours are not physically present. They most often arise from the *apparent* partial occlusion of a set of objects by a surface closer in depth to the observer. In this sense, not only contours but illusory figures can emerge. The apparently occluding surface appears lighter than the homogeneous surface of which it is physically a part, just as a region of constant lightness appears lighter when perceived as figure than when seen as ground in ambiguous figure-ground stimuli (see Unit 2.2). Illusory contours illustrate that the perception of parts of a stimulus can depend on the configuration of the stimulus as a whole.

Interaction 2.3.4 illustrates a second class of illusory contours, those deriving from a shift in phase between horizontal lines. The change in phase is interpreted as resulting from partial occlusion of one part of the field by another. This entails perception of an implicit difference in depth between parts of the field. Study the examples in this interaction carefully, noting the apparent occlusion (which surface appears to obscure which) and corresponding differences in apparent depth within the field. These phase-induced illusory contours demonstrate that subjective contours are not contingent upon the existence of luminance gradients within the stimulus or field.

The left-most example of the four given in Interaction 2.3.4 is particularly interesting for another reason. It neatly illustrates figure-ground reversal of the kind explored in Unit 2.2. Note how the curved illusory contour attaches to the *figure*—the apparently closer of the two halves of the square field—changing "allegiance" each time figure and ground reverse.

Illusory contours pose an interesting theoretical dilemma for perceptual psychologists. The best that can be said, for the moment, is that some interesting partial theories exist; certainly there is no compelling explanation of the phenomenon. Schiffman (1996) provides a lucid review of some of the competing theories, which you may find particularly helpful. One explanation (based on lightness contrast effects) suggests that illusory contours are the edges of an area that appears brighter than its background because of the existence of steep lightness gradients in that region. This idea is at odds, however, with the illusory contours used in Interaction 2.3.4, which are generated by phase-shifts in horizontal line gratings (for versions of these contrast explanations, see Frisby & Clatworthy, 1975; Jory & Day, 1979; Frisby, 1980).

Coren (1972) has suggested that illusory contours are generated when the perceptual system reinterprets and simplifies a complex, improbable, two dimensional array of stimulus elements. In essence, the 2-D array is transformed into a coherent, integrated, meaningful, and inherently simpler configuration by reinterpreting the elements such that they are part of a *three*-dimensional array. The illusory contour generated is the edge of one plane apparently separated in depth from a second plane under this 3-D construction of the stimulus field. Rock (1986) has demonstrated, however, that the difference in apparent depth typically emerges *after* perception of the figure with illusory contours. There, nevertheless, appears to be a strong cognitive-interpretive element in the genesis of illusory contours. They appear to be what Rock has called a *cognitive invention.* The susceptibility of apparent contours to factors such as priming, instructions, familiarity, and perceptual set suggest there may be a substantial cognitive component in such illusions.

As noted, the apparently occluding surface appears lighter than the homogeneous, equireflectance surface of which it is physically a part, just as a region of constant lightness appears lighter when perceived as figure than when seen as ground in ambiguous figure-ground stimuli. Indeed, one account of illusory contours is based on the fact that the figure generally appears lighter than a ground of equivalent lightness (Bradley & Dumais, 1975; Dumais & Bradley, 1976; Bradley & Petry,

1977). This suggests that the anomalous lightness of surfaces defined by illusory contours is wholly due to the fact that they are seen as figure. The lightness effect is subordinate to, and derived from, the perception of figure.

It is important to note that illusory contours seem not to be generated if the apparently occluded inducing shapes or elements are themselves apparently coherent and complete high-probability shapes. In other words, if the inducing shapes appear not to be occluded by an illusory central surface, then illusory contours are not perceived and no such surface emerges.

It appears that the roots of illusory contours may lie in the perceptual tendency expressed in the Gestalt law of Pragnänz (sometimes called the law of simplicity, or the law of good figure); Coren's explanation of illusory contours, in particular, invokes this principle. So, try to tie the explorations in this unit back to the Gestalt principles outlined in Unit 2.1.

However subjective contours are ultimately explained, it seems likely that cognitive mediation, interpretation, or invention will be seen to play a significant role.

Computer technology can be used to generate unusual dynamic illusory contours. **Interactions 2.3.1**, **2.3.3**, and **2.3.5**, for instance, demonstrate some fascinating examples of the illusory contours generated when the shape and/or size of the apparently occluding surface are continuously transformed, or when that surface appears to be in constant motion.

Subjective contours are not simply all-or-none phenomena: in **Interaction 2.3.2**, for example, you can explore how they can vary widely in subjective strength or intensity, depending on the nature, distribution, and number of inducing elements. You may find it interesting to speculate and experiment a little, trying to come up with optimal inducing fields.

In **Interaction 2.3.6** you will see that strong illusory contours can be generated via the apparent occlusion of "real-world" objects. That interaction also illustrates the fact that illusory surfaces have many of the same properties as actual surfaces. We use them in this interaction to generate illusions.

Unit 2.4 Figural Aftereffects and Textural Contours

2.4.5 Factors in Textural Segregation
2.4.6 Textons and Contour Strength

Prolonged inspection of a figure, or constellation of elements, can often result in misperception or distortion of a subsequently viewed figure. Experimental psychology provides many fascinating examples of these *figural aftereffects.* In **Interaction 2.4.1**, you can explore one of the more famous, an aftereffect initially reported by Köhler and Wallach in 1944. Prolonged inspection of a pattern of squares causes an apparent distortion, or displacement, in the spatial distribution of squares in a subsequently presented test pattern.

There have been several different attempts to explain figural aftereffects, few of much theoretical interest. The earliest attempts at explanation—based on postulated cortical electrical fields and, later, eye movements—bordered on the mystical. The cortical electrical fields were shown not to exist and eye movements were demonstrated to be irrelevant. Similar explanations have invoked notions of receptor "satiation" and subsequent displacement of images from the satiated region of the retina—indeed, Köhler and Wallach themselves invoked this kind of explanation. You may feel uncomfortable with this kind of explanation, in that it amounts to little more than a redescription of the observed phenomenon in quasiphysiological terms.

Figural aftereffects are now usually explained in terms of the adaptation of multiple spatial frequency channels along the lines sketched by Blakemore & Sutton (1969). They had observers inspect low and high frequency gratings for some time and then tested them with medium frequency gratings. Adaptation to high frequency gratings caused subsequent gratings to be perceived as lower frequency than they were, and vice versa. You can test this phenomenon for yourself in **Interaction 4.8.2**.

In general terms, multiple channel theory suggests that there are multiple channels concerned with the detection of gratings, or patterns, each tuned to detect—respond maximally to—a particular spatial frequency. These channels selectively fatigue, or adapt, during prolonged inspection of a grating. The channel corresponding most closely to the inspection grating will be most affected and become least responsive—although the output of similar-frequency channels may also be depressed. During subsequent exposure to a test grating, output from that channel(s) is selectively depressed and the resulting output pattern, or activity profile, from the channels is distorted, resulting in misperception.

Because the mechanisms underlying aftereffects are relatively poorly understood, attempts to classify or type them are sometimes conflicting and seldom very satisfying. One such classification, or typology, identifies figural, shape, and contingent aftereffects. Tilt aftereffects of the kind illustrated in **Interaction 2.4.2** are usually thought of as a special class of figural aftereffect (although some theorists would argue that the notion of figural aftereffect is somewhat dated and should be replaced). **Interaction 2.4.3** provides you with the opportunity to explore an unusual example of a shape aftereffect. Shape aftereffects typically subsume so-called curvature aftereffects. A shape aftereffect is said to occur when prolonged inspection of a form, or shape, results in distortion of a subsequently presented test shape. Exposure to curved contours, for example, can make subsequently presented straight lines appear curved in the opposite direction.

Contingent aftereffects are not dealt with in this unit, but you can explore a powerful example—the McCollough effect—in Interaction 3.8.6. Contingent aftereffects demonstrate that it is possible to selectively adapt to two or three stimulus properties in combination and, moreover, that the aftereffect to one of the properties can be contingent upon the presence of the other(s). For instance—as is the case with the McCollough effect—observers can experience different color aftereffects depending on the orientation of a test grid after prolonged exposure to stimuli with different color-orientation pairings. This is generally consistent with the notion that there are channels of the visual system tuned for both orientation and color. Similar contingencies can exist between color and shape, color and curvature, and color and direction of movement. In these cases, the color aftereffects experienced are said to be shape, curvature, or motion contingent.

Interaction 2.4.4 provides a powerful demonstration that form and motion are processed separately in the early stages of perception. This interaction presents shapes that, paradoxically, do not exist at any given moment. They consist of smaller random squares indistinguishable from a random-dot background. You will see the square only when it is in motion; it disappears instantaneously when stopped. The motion system deduces the existence of the square by cross-correlating the changing images over time. This interaction provides evidence that, although form and motion are processed separately, the former receives input from the latter. Make sure you check out the closely related random-dot kinematogram in Interaction 2.7.2.

Units 2.1 and 2.2 dealt extensively with the perception of forms, shapes, or figures and the discrimination of figure from ground. In those units, forms were usually defined by differences in wavelength (hue) or brightness. Object boundaries can also be defined by differences in *visual texture*. In general, texture refers to the apparent roughness or graininess of a figure or ground—its microstructure of contour elements or shapes. Texture is independent of—that is, not reliant on differences in—brightness or color. Textural differences can set regions apart or be used as a cue in separating figure from ground. The boundary between regions of different texture is termed a *textural contour*. These textural contours can be thought of as a class of subjective, or illusory, contour; the perceived contour is not physically present. In this sense, you can conceptually relate the material on textural contours in **Interactions 2.4.5** and **2.4.6** to the quite extensive explorations of illusory contours in Unit 2.2.

Not all shapes defined by textural differences are equally discriminable, of course. Note in Interaction 2.4.6, for instance, that the textural diamond made up of triangles is rather difficult to discriminate in the absence of color differences between figure and ground. Study that example carefully and try to establish what unique factors are at work. Eye movements certainly appear to be necessary to isolate figure from ground.

The process whereby we isolate, or perceptually separate, regions or fields differing in visual texture is called *textural segregation*. Again, this process is related to principles addressed elsewhere in *Exploring Perception*. Textural segregation may be thought of as a special case of Gestalt grouping by similarity (Interaction 2.1.2), although predictions of textural segregation based on naive definitions of similarity, at least, are occasionally disconfirmed (see Coren et al., 1994, pp. 282–283).

You will come across the notion of *textons* from time to time (Julesz & Bergen, 1983). These can be thought of as the properties, or features, of the local elements that together compose a texture—including their orientations, shapes, lengths, line crossings, terminators—that operate at the preattentive stages of vision to cause textural segregation. These are the primitives for object perception and textural segregation. Clear differences in the class, number, density, or distribution of these textons will make textural segregation relatively easy. Coren et al. (1994, pp. 282–284) provide a brief, interesting, and helpful discussion of the issues raised by the last two interactions in this unit, and I recommend it to you.

Unit 2.5 The Phi Phenomenon

At the heart of Gestalt psychology is the notion that the perceptual whole is somehow more than—or, at least, different from—the sum of its parts. As noted in Unit 2.1, Gestaltists have argued that there appear to be emergent properties of perceptual objects, which are not readily explicable in terms of the constituent parts from which they derive. Unit 2.5 explores this general principle in the domain of apparent movement.

All of the interactions in this unit have the same underlying structure. You are able to rapidly alternate two frames, or pictures, in which an object in frame 1 is more or less displaced in frame 2, thus generating apparent movement. The contents of each frame can be checked manually and you will find it useful to examine them before launching into an interaction proper.

It is also possible to manually alternate the frames. In this way, you will come to understand precisely how the various apparent movement phenomena are being generated. Gestaltists would argue, then, that the apparent movement you will encounter in this unit is an emergent property. The perceived stimulus is not only moving, when the frames are merely still pictures, but it is often seen in the space between its locations in the two frames—where no stimulus object physically exists.

You may find it useful to remind yourself, from time to time, that the movement you are witnessing is illusory and return to analyze precisely the stimulus configurations generating it. The general principle at work in all of these apparent movement interactions is the same as that used to make moving pictures. As Bruce Goldstein notes (1996, p. 293), it is curious that, although the motion picture industry began to flourish in the early 1900s, it wasn't until about 1912 that psychologists began to study apparent movement in earnest.

The theoretical importance of apparent movement in those early days of experimental psychology lay in the commentary it provided on the prevailing Germanic structuralist ideology. Taking their line from the physical sciences in general, and chemistry in particular, the structuralists—led by Wilhelm Wundt's student Edward Bradford Titchener—had argued that all conscious experience arose from sensation-elements, to which all complex mental experience or perceptions could be reduced. The Gestaltists, Max Wertheimer in particular, were able to point to apparent movement as a phenomenon not reducible to elementary atomistic sensations. They were able to show—principally via the *phi phenomenon*—that, although apparent movement derives from simple sensations, it cannot be reduced to them. It is interesting to note, perhaps, that Wertheimer used Wolfgang Köhler and Kurt Koffka, both 25 years old at the time, as his subjects during those first experiments on the phi phenomenon in 1912. Both were to become outstanding Gestalt psychologists.

Interaction 2.5.1 enables you to investigate the phi phenomenon in some detail. That interaction, and a number of others in this unit, allows you to vary the lateral separation of the corresponding elements in the two frames and the interframe interval, which governs the rate of alternation of the two pictures. Try to spend time investigating the trade-off relationship between these two key variables and the way they impact perceived motion.

It is important to "tune" these variables very carefully in Interaction 2.5.1, in particular, to observe objectless movement, partial movement, and the fully developed phi phenomenon. If the interframe interval is too brief, the spheres will be seen in their correct locations simultaneously. If it is too long, you will see one sphere followed by the other in the second location. Depending on the settings you use, you should be able to observe phi, optimum, and partial movement.

Partial movement is usually seen at short interframe intervals, becoming optimum movement (the sphere moves continuously in the spaces between its locations in the separate frames) as that interval is increased. At longer interframe intervals still, *phi* or *objectless* movement is usually observed; there is an impression of movement, but it is difficult to see the object moving in the space between its frame locations.

Interaction 2.5.2 nicely illustrates a Gestalt principle at work in addition to apparent movement. When two vertically separated elements are horizontally displaced in the second of two rapidly alternating frames, their apparent movement is always horizontal. So, although it is theoretically possible that the elements' paths might cross—that is, that they might be seen to move diagonally—this is seldom, if ever, observed. When two or more perceptual possibilities exist, human subjects tend to see the simpler, more parsimonious option. You may recognize this as the Gestalt law of simplicity or good figure.

We see the Gestalt law of meaningfulness at work in **Interaction 2.5.3**, which powerfully illustrates the constructive and inferential nature of perception. When a barrier is interposed in the path of an apparently moving object, that object can appear to "jump" over, or under, the barrier. Its path, in that case, appears bowed or curved, despite the fact that its theoretical trajectory is linear.

There is a tendency, then, to perceive the simplest, most plausible, or meaningful construction of an improbable and complex stimulus pattern. In a sense, bowed movement is "inferred" (though not necessarily consciously). The moving object appears to jump the barrier because, in the real world, substantial objects cannot pass *through* an apparently solid barrier. Interpretation of the stimulus pattern in those terms would be implausible.

You can see the constructive and inferential nature of perception at work again in **Interaction 2.5.4**, where the phenomenon of split movement is explored. Again, the perceptual-cognitive system is challenged to "make sense" of an improbable and conflicting stimulus pattern. A vertical green block is rapidly alternated in time and space with two horizontal blocks. What possible real-world configuration could be giving rise to this pattern of stimulation? Once the stimulus parameters are satisfactorily tuned, the vertical block will appear to split in two and counterrotate to two new (horizontal) locations.

It is important not to take these rational-cognitive reconstructions of perceptual events too literally. Although you may find this approach has some heuristic, or analytical, value for you, remember that the actual processes involved are poorly understood. The perceptual experiences involved tend to be instantaneous and automatic rather than consciously rational or cognitive.

Interaction 2.5.5 is interesting insofar as it shows how the phenomenon of apparent movement may be used to shed light on other issues of theoretical importance. For instance, the human visual system can extract salient features from complex displays rapidly and monitor only those features in subsequent images, thus speeding up perceptual processing. In this interaction, you can use apparent motion to check whether your visual system processes brightness before it processes edges and sharp outlines.

This theme is extended somewhat in **Interaction 2.5.6**, which provides the opportunity to check what happens when apparent movement is induced between two stimuli that have a different color or shape. What we know is that the perceived stimulus must be transformed in some way if it is to retain its identity as a single, but displaced, object. It is of some theoretical importance whether that transition, or transformation, is gradual and continuous, or abrupt. Interaction 2.5.6 should provide an interesting demonstration that shape and size appear to be continuously transformed, whereas color changes tend to be abrupt and *all or none* (although this is not always the case).

Unit 2.6 Contextual Effects and Apparent Movement

2.6.1 Path-Guided Apparent Motion
2.6.2 Apparent Motion and Figural Selection
2.6.3 Apparent Motion and Experience

This unit extends the material covered in Unit 2.5 to explore a range of more complex apparent movement phenomena generally known as *field effects* and *contextual effects.* All of the interactions in this unit exemplify the operation of the Gestalt principles dealt with elsewhere in this module. None of the perceptual experiences dealt with in Unit 2.6 is easily analyzed, or explained, in terms of elementary sensory experiences. All exemplify the importance of the perceptual whole, or Gestalt, in determining perceptual experience. Emergent properties appear to be implicated in all of the interactions in this unit.

Interaction 2.6.1 is an interesting case in point. Apparent movement usually takes the shortest route between the successive spatially distinct locations of a stimulus in a sequence of frames. In this interaction, it is shown that a perceptual object in apparent motion can seem to take a curved, rather than linear, path under certain conditions. As you will see, if a dim curved band is flashed in the interval between frames, it is possible for perceptual objects to appear to travel extremely curved paths. The visual system integrates the stimulus sequence into a "satisfying" (if ultimately misleading) perceptual experience.

Interaction 2.6.2 contrasts the split movement explored in Interaction 2.5.4 with the phenomenon of *figural selection*. Again, you will see the constructive and inferential nature of perception at work. You will see what happens when the perceptual-cognitive system is challenged to "make sense" of an improbable and somewhat conflicting stimulus pattern. It is important that you carefully analyze the contents of the frames generating the apparent movement as you move through the interaction.

Initially, a vertical green block is rapidly alternated in time with two horizontal blocks. Once the stimulus parameters are satisfactorily tuned, the vertical block will appear to split in two and counterrotate to two new (horizontal) locations. In the figural selection condition, however, the stimulus is changed such that frame 2 now contains laterally displaced horizontal and vertical blocks.

Three possibilities present themselves. Will the vertical block in frame 1 (i) rotate to merge with the horizontal block; (ii) move to the right to merge with the vertical block; or (iii) split to merge with both? In this case, as Paul Kolers showed, apparent movement occurs only toward the more similar (vertical) rectangle in frame 2—even when it is the more distant. Kolers called this phenomenon *figural selection.*

As you will discover, figural selection takes precedence over split movement. Again, the system appears to interpret the stimuli in the simplest, most parsimonious way—a Gestalt principle we have seen exemplified in a range of disparate stimulus conditions.

One might expect that perceptual experiences with a substantial constructive, top-down component might be susceptible to change via learning or experience. Indeed, Max Wertheimer, the earliest systematic investigator of apparent movement, was particularly interested in the role played by past experience in the perception of *phi* and related phenomena. **Interaction 2.6.3** is an approximate reconstruction of an experiment carried out by Wertheimer as early as 1912. It should lead you to much the same conclusion that he reached: the perception of apparent movement can be influenced by an observer's immediately prior experience.

Gestalt psychologists have long argued that consideration of the properties of an object, or element, in isolation may be insufficient to understand the perceptual experience to which it (in context) gives rise. One must take into account the whole perceptual field, because the relationships between elements can be critical. This precept underpinned discussion of many of the interactions in Units 2.1 and 2.2, particularly in those interactions concerned with the *laws of organization*. Just as context—the configuration of elements in the perceptual field—can govern the grouping of stationary elements, it can also play a role in determining what is perceived when those elements are in apparent motion. **Interaction 2.6.4** provides a compelling example. If several elements in a field move in unison in entrained, or harnessed, apparent motion, a given element can be seen to move, even when it is not present in the second of the two alternating frames generating that apparent motion.

In several interactions in this module there appears to be a tendency to use simplifying inferences to interpret improbable stationary stimulus patterns. The motion system uses simplifying inferences in much the same way. This property occasionally causes us to perceive movement when none is present, and to make unusual "higher-order" interpretations of simple movement. In **Interaction 2.6.5**, for instance, one might predict that the trash can in frame 1 will appear to move toward the can in frame 2 and fuse with it, while the rat remains stationary, blinking on and off. In fact, most observers tend to see the rat move behind the trash can—an example of a higher-order, apparently cognitive, inference, in which the "meaning" of the stimulus elements plays a role.

In the real world, converging objects either collide or pass, they tend not to merge per se. In this sense, the rat-and-trash can scenario is a plausible construction of the improbable stimulus events distributed in time and space. It is not clear the extent to which the processes involved here are properly termed *rational* or *cognitive*; so, again, take care not to be too literal in your thinking about the inferential processes that might be at work. At best they might be termed quasi-rational or quasi-cognitive.

Interaction 2.6.6 is an interesting example of how apparent motion can be reinterpreted in the light of changes in configuration, or context. A stimulus apparently moving diagonally comes to be seen to move horizontally if its ultimate "destination" is occluded. All this, despite the fact that no stimulus ever occupies that putative destination.

Unit 2.7 Phenomenal Identity and Movement Aftereffects

A major problem in providing a comprehensive account of motion perception is to explain how the relentless cascade of ever-changing retinal images—generated by the often-simultaneous movement of body, head, eyes, and objects—is transformed into a stable representation of the world. How does our visual system detect, for instance, that an object at one moment in time is the same as the object that we see a moment later in a different location? That is, how do we solve the problem of correspondence?

Most of the apparent movement interactions in this module have been concerned with the simple motion of one or two elements or multiple discrete elements in harnessed or entrained motion. Adding elements to apparently moving arrays can give rise to some complex and unexpected perceptual effects. **Interaction 2.7.1**, for instance, reproduces the essentials of an early experiment by Ternus—discussed in some detail by Goldstein (1989, pp. 289-290)—and a more recent extension of it by Pantle and Picciano (1976).

This experiment neatly exemplifies some of the Gestalt principles that have been the recurrent theme of this module. First and foremost, it illustrates (again) how important the overall configuration of a stimulus field is in determining the nature of a perceptual event. In particular, it shows that the interstimulus (or interframe) interval can dramatically affect what is seen.

Note that there is another example of the importance of this variable in Interaction 2.5.1 where, depending on the interframe interval used, you should be able to observe phi, optimum, or partial movement.

By carefully adjusting the interframe interval in Interaction 2.7.1, you will probably observe two dramatically different effects, related to the phenomenal identity of the individual elements. Begin by noting carefully the contents of each frame. Each contains three dots. The two left-most dots in frame 2 overlap with the two right-most dots in frame 1. At longer interframe intervals, you will probably notice three dots in what is called *group movement*—they oscillate back and forth, as a group, retaining a unified and stable identity in entrained movement.

It is useful to note here, as elsewhere, that the perceptual whole is different from the sum of its parts. Only two of the dots are common to the two frames. The identity is, in fact, illusory. Pantle and Picciano reproduced this group movement, or phenomenal identity, at longer interstimulus intervals (ISIs); but, at very short ISIs, observers reported seeing the two overlapping elements in each frame as stationary, while the third dot moved back-and-forth from one end of the array to the other. This is usually referred to as *element,* as opposed to *group*, movement. With luck, you should be able to observe both group and element movement in Interaction 1.7.1.

These data suggest that there are two different mechanisms, or systems, for apparent movement—one tapped at each interframe interval. If you are interested in following this through, Bruce Goldstein (1989, pp. 291–295) examines other evidence for these two systems. He makes the point that, although form and movement are linked in our consciousness, there is some evidence that the two qualities are processed separately in the slow *low-level system* (tapped in this interaction at the longer interframe intervals). The random-dot kinematogram in **Interaction 2.7.2** provides a nice illustration of this point (as does the very similar contour-from-motion demonstration in Interaction 2.4.4).

Interaction 2.7.3 illustrates a second class of apparent movement called *induced movement*. What is in motion is not always perceived as being in motion. If an object in motion is perceived to be still, the appearance of movement can be induced in a nearby object. Induced motion is usually, but not necessarily, rectilinear. Occasionally, circular motion is induced, for example.

In Interaction 2.7.3, apparent movement of the airplane is induced by the impression of movement of the sky and clouds, which form the background—or frame of reference—for the plane. Typically, movement is induced in a smaller (or enclosed) object by a moving larger (or enclosing) object. We encounter many examples of induced movement in everyday life: that experienced when seated in a stationary train being passed by a slowly moving train; the stationary moon appearing to scud through moving clouds; and so on.

In essence, induced movement is a visual illusion: there is movement—or the impression of movement—in the perceptual field, but it is attached to the wrong element in the stimulus array.

In complex arrays, with several elements in each frame, there appear to be some general principles, or rules, governing the kind of apparent movement perceived. When multiple possibilities exist, there is a tendency to see motion that (i) requires the slowest speed; (ii) covers the shortest path; and (iii) preserves the configuration and rigidity of three-dimensional objects [for a succinct summary and detailed references see Coren et al. (1994, p. 462)]. These factors clearly play an important role in the way the correspondence problem, outlined earlier, is solved. There is, nevertheless, a degree of tolerance or flexibility and room for a good deal of higher-order interpretation of complex, ambiguous stimulus patterns. This module provides many examples of these kinds of processes in operation.

Interaction 2.7.4, based on the work of Ramchandran and Anstis (1986), is a particularly powerful demonstration of several inferential and interpretive processes simultaneously being brought to bear on the resolution of a complex stimulus pattern. Not only is movement observed when none exists, but that apparent movement is of an *illusory* surface. Moreover, that illusory surface appears to “capture” the wholly stationary background dots and carry them with it. Thus, both the subjective surface and dots appear to move back and forth, in the total absence of any movement of elements across the retina. There are many instances in this module of higher-order cognitive (top-down) processes at work in motion perception, but none is more striking than that in Interaction 2.7.4.

The last two interactions in this unit (**Interactions 2.7.5** and **2.7.6**) provide examples of motion aftereffects at work. These phenomena are interesting in their own right, but their importance for psychologists and neuroscientists lies in the insights they provide into possible neural mechanisms of movement perception. There is some evidence of retinal ganglion cells in rabbit and frog eyes that respond to movement of a stimulus in one direction only. In the higher animals (for example, monkeys and cats) there are no directionally sensitive retinal cells, but good evidence for cells of that class in the visual cortex. The existence of movement aftereffects in humans suggested that similar cells may exist in the human visual system and play an important role in motion perception. There is now some neurophysiological evidence that such cells do, in fact, exist.

The waterfall illusion, an analog of which is incorporated in Interaction 2.7.5, is a classic example of a movement aftereffect. When gaze is shifted after prolonged observation of the cascade of a waterfall, observers typically see stationary objects in the visual field drifting upward. There is some suggestion (Peter Wenderoth, personal communication) that this aftereffect is eliminated completely if the moving test bars and stationary surround bars are perfectly aligned when the moving bars stop! This will occasionally be the case in this interaction, so check out Professor Wenderoth's hypothesis.

Movement aftereffects are usually explained in terms of adaptation, fatigue, or satiation of direction-specific motion detectors—that is, cells tuned to detect a specific direction of movement. Because these aftereffects are transferred interocularly (exposure to movement in one eye can result in a movement aftereffect in the other) we know that the locus of such effects is not at the retina, but higher in the visual system, where the images from the two eyes are recombined (that is, the visual cortex).

In the case of the waterfall illusion, cells tuned to detect downward movement become progressively less sensitive after prolonged stimulation. When gaze is shifted, the output of other-direction motion detectors (including upward-motion detectors) will be greater than that of the fatigued downward-motion detectors. In the absence of a countervailing downward-motion signal, elements in the field of view will be interpreted (perceived) to be drifting upward. You might be interested in comparing this class of explanation with that outlined for figural aftereffects in Unit 2.4.

Unit 2.8 Motion Detection, Apparent Velocity, and Causation

A complicating factor in motion perception is the fact that, at any moment, the body, head, and eyes can be moving as well as the target object. To make sense of the kaleidoscopic stimulation on the retinae, kinaesthetic feedback is vital. Much use is made of the efferent signals sent to control eye movement.

Occasionally, kinesthetic feedback is inadequate, incorrect, or too slow, and this can give rise to misperceptions or motion illusions—the *autokinetic effect*, for example. It is thought to derive from (among other things) the interaction of involuntary eye movements and impoverished viewing conditions. With involuntary eye movement, the retinal location of an image changes, but there are no corresponding efferent signals that the motion detection system can use to "discount" the change in the retinal location of the stationary target object; it appears to move spontaneously and haphazardly.

Interaction 2.8.1 provides an opportunity to explore another, related class of motion illusion, based on the work of Festinger and Easton (1974). Being naturally limited in velocity, smooth pursuit eye movements can lag behind a moving target, giving rise to velocity-related distortions, or illusions, in the apparent path traced by that object. At very slow velocities, an object is relatively easily tracked and path-perception is accurate. Similarly, at very fast object velocities, when smooth pursuit is not possible, the object's path is seen accurately. In Interaction 2.8.1, the actual path of the red dot remains square at all times. At intermediate velocities, however, when tracking lags behind the object, distinctive velocity-related movement illusions are experienced. The illusory paths usually seen are illustrated in the interaction. The illusion is attributable to the fact that, when tracking lags, the efferent signals are not accurately reflecting the true location of the red dot at all times. Movement illusions are exacerbated in sparse or impoverished viewing conditions.

The last two interactions in Unit 2.7 were concerned with the movement-opposite aftereffects generated by prolonged inspection of movement in a fixed direction. These aftereffects are generally consistent with the existence of direction-specific motion detection cells in the visual system. The *phantom grating* generated in **Interaction 2.8.2** provides additional evidence for direction-sensitive motion detectors. The critical point to note here is that the phantom grating disappears when movement of the inducing grating is stopped—evidence that the motion detection system is implicated.

Tynan and Sekuler (1975), on whose work Interaction 2.8.2 is based, went beyond our simple demonstration. They noted that the phantom grating disappeared if either the top or the bottom "prongs" were covered (you might try this and check their finding). More important, if the top of the grating was delivered to the right eye and the bottom to the left eye, phantom gratings were seen. The logic used in discussing movement aftereffects applies again here: the effects observed cannot be retinal. The locus of the effect must be higher in the visual system, where the images from the two eyes are recombined—namely, the visual cortex.

It is not surprising that we are able to invoke a similar logic to explain phantom gratings and movement aftereffects: it appears that precisely the same direction-specific motion detectors may be involved in the two phenomena. In fact, strong motion aftereffects are generated by the same stimulus conditions that generate phantom gratings (Weisstein, Maguire, & Berbaum, 1977). You will find a nice summary of the relationship between motion aftereffects and phantom gratings—and related issues in motion detection—in Levine and Shefner (1991, pp. 366–381).

The perceived velocity of a moving stimulus depends not only on its rate of displacement, but on the context, or frame of reference, in which that movement is taking place. For instance, the size of the field in which an object is moving can markedly affect its apparent velocity—as **Interaction 2.8.3** clearly demonstrates. The smaller the field of movement, the greater the apparent velocity of a moving object. But there is a confound in this demonstration (field size is not the only the factor varied). Can you identify that confound? Would you expect it to play a significant role? Why? Relate this issue to Question 1 in the quiz for this interaction.

Contextual factors other than field size can play an important role in determining apparent velocity. The relationship between the speed of the image across the retina and its apparent speed. For instance, in **Interaction 2.8.4**, the apparent speed of the constant-speed soccer ball increases as it approaches either end of the reference box in which it moves. This interaction is an analog of an early study by Brown (1931). He showed that a small object was also speeded as it approached and crossed under a central fixation string.

Interaction 2.8.5, illustrating the phenomenon of *velocity transposition*, is also based on an early study by Brown (1931b). Brown had subjects adjust the speed of a large dot moving in a large rectangle so that it appeared to be traveling at the same rate as a small dot in a small rectangle. When the larger rectangle was ten times the size of the smaller, the former had to move at seven times the speed of the latter to appear to be traveling at the same speed. Analogously, a cat in a large cage must move faster than a mouse in a small cage to be seen to be moving at the same speed.

Bruce Goldstein (1989, p. 279) provides a nice example of the effect of velocity transposition at work in our perception of moving pictures.

Imagine that a car drives from left to right across the screen in 3 seconds. On a much larger screen (with the film projected from a greater distance) it still takes 3 seconds. The image is moving more quickly across the large screen, but does the car appear to be traveling faster? No. Velocity transposition is at work.

Not only does context affect the apparent velocity of objects, it is a vital factor in determining motion detection thresholds.

Module 3

Perceiving Color

Unit 3.1 Color and Wavelength

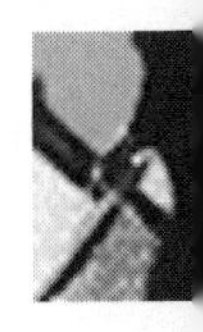

Light is the stimulus for vision. It can be thought of as traveling in waves; light is just one tiny sliver of the spectrum of electromagnetic energy, which includes gamma rays, x-rays, television and radio waves, and many other kinds of electromagnetic radiation. Each has a distinctive wavelength. Electromagnetic radiation varies in wavelength from a few trillionths of a meter to several kilometers. **Interaction 3.1.1** shows where visible light falls in the spectrum of electromagnetic energy and locates the other familiar classes of electromagnetic radiation. The locations shown are only approximate, particularly in that part of the spectrum dedicated to radio and television signals. There is some variation from country to country; FM signals, for instance, sometimes fall into the television band.

Although not all light is visible—we cannot see infrared or ultraviolet light, for instance—radiation with wavelengths between about 360 and 780 nanometers stimulates receptors in our retinae and gives rise to visual sensations. Sir Isaac Newton demonstrated that so-called white light (for example, sunlight) is a mixture of all the wavelengths in this range. In a now classical experiment, he was able to separate white light into its component wavelengths using a glass refracting prism, because of the property that the prism refracted the light waves by an amount inversely proportional to their wavelength. Short wavelengths, corresponding to the blue end of the spectrum were refracted most, whereas the longer wavelengths—usually seen as reds—were refracted least. When projected onto a white screen, the various wavelengths of light (or spectral energy bands) created the impression of spatially distinct bands of color.

So, different wavelengths of visible light create different color impressions. For instance, 500-nanometer electromagnetic radiation falling on the retina will typically give rise to the sensation of green, and 573-nanometer light will usually be seen as yellow. Remember, the light itself is not colored. It gives rise to the impression of color only when it falls on specialized photoreceptors in the eye, called *cones,* and gives rise to electrical signals subsequently interpreted by the brain. Thus, color is a psychological phenomenon, not a property of the light rays falling on the retina.

So, take care in interpreting **Interactions 3.1.2** and **3.1.3**, in particular; they map spectral colors to particular wavelengths of light. Remember that light of a given wavelength evokes a particular color impression; it cannot be said to possess color in its own right.

Further, color is a private, subjective experience, as **Interaction 3.1.6** makes clear. You cannot know precisely the color experienced by another person when his or her cones are stimulated by, say, 450-nanometer (nm) light. The wavelength of light energy estimated to evoke the impression of purest green, for instance, will vary from person to person. Again, in a very real sense, colors are *created* by our nervous systems; they are not a property of light of a particular wavelength. In general terms, however, knowing the wavelength of light stimulating the eye of a color-normal observer will give us a good idea of the color impression experienced by that person. The wavelength of light energy is the physical property most closely corresponding to the impression of color.

It is important not to confuse spectral red (which has a slight tinge of yellow) with so-called unique red. Unique red, a red that contains no trace of any other color, is nonspectral. It is achieved by adding a small quantity of 400-nm blue to spectral red. Thus, the psychologically purest red is not monochromatic, but a mixture—an *extraspectral* color.

The colors of opaque objects are dependent on the wavelengths of the light they *reflect* to the eye of the observer. Different objects reflect different amounts of the light of each wavelength falling on them. If the percentage of light reflected by an object is plotted as a function of the wavelength of that light, the result is called the *reflectance curve* for that object. **Interaction 3.1.4** gives you the opportunity to explore the reflectance curves of several common objects. The important point to note is that real-world objects don't selectively reflect a single wavelength, or even a narrow band of wavelengths. In general terms, achromatic objects tend to reflect light evenly across the spectrum. Objects seen to have chromatic colors, selectively reflect only some wavelengths in the spectrum, but across quite a wide range. If objects *reflect* only some wavelengths, it is important to keep in mind that they *absorb* the rest.

In the case of translucent objects, such as glass (or some fluids or plastics), their color is determined by the wavelengths of light they selectively *transmit,* rather than reflect. For example, strawberry soda selectively transmits the longer wavelengths of light energy, that are seen as reddish. The other side of this coin, of course, is that strawberry soda absorbs all wavelengths except those usually seen as red. In this sense, the soda acts as a filter, subtracting the short and medium wavelengths from the white illuminating light—which has equal intensity at all wavelengths. **Interaction 3.1.5** assists you in exploring the color a translucent object, or fluid, will have if it selectively transmits short, medium, and/or long wavelengths. It is important that you understand why translucent substances have the colors they do.

In general terms, then, this unit is designed to provide you with an appreciation of the nature of electromagnetic energy as the stimulus for vision, and the relationship between the wavelength of electromagnetic energy falling on the retina and the perception of color. You will find it useful to know roughly which wavelengths give rise to which color impressions. Be sure you understand why solid and translucent objects have the colors they do, and be aware of the sense in which the perception of color is a private experience.

Unit 3.2 Hue, Brightness, and Saturation

3.2.1 The Color Circle
3.2.2 Saturation
3.2.3 Hue and Saturation
3.2.4 Hue and Brightness
3.2.5 The Color Spindle
3.2.6 Perceived Color and the Color Spindle

This unit provides an overview of the psychological dimensions along which color is said to vary and illustrates two, related, spatial models of color: the color circle and the color spindle. These perceptual dimensions of color are directly related—in consistent and measurable ways—to physical properties of the electromagnetic energy that is the stimulus for vision.

It is sometimes useful to describe visible light, which may be thought of as being made up of waves, in terms of the physical properties of those waves: their wavelength, wave amplitude, and purity. When light waves fall on the retina and are transduced into electrical signals that ultimately reach the brain, they give rise to visual perceptions—to psychological experiences. One such perception is *hue*, which is related, in part, to the wavelength(s) of the light falling on the retina. So, hue or color is the psychological attribute, or property, that most closely corresponds to variations in wavelength.

In general, perceived hue varies as the wavelengths that are contained in the light stimulus vary. So, it is possible (approximately) to specify a hue, or color, in terms of the spectral composition of the light that gives rise to it. Colors such as gray, black, and white are termed *achromatic* colors, whereas those such as red, yellow, and green are called *chromatic colors*. The term *hue* is usually reserved for chromatic colors. In fact, we seldom use the term hue and usually refer simply to the *color* red or the *color* blue. In this module, we use the term *color* to mean *chromatic color* or *hue*.

There is no simple one-to-one relationship between the physical stimulus, the spectral composition of the light falling on the retina, and the psychological experience of color that it evokes. Perception is a private, and sometimes idiosyncratic, experience. Color experience is, then, the psychological or subjective effect of activity in the nervous system, not a property of the electromagnetic radiation (light) itself.

Light waves vary in amplitude—that is, in the height or displacement of their peaks—as well as in wavelength. In general, light waves with greater amplitude are perceived as brighter. It is important to note that, strictly, a light is not bright. It is simply that large-amplitude waves look bright—they evoke a perception of brightness in the observer. In the same way, light waves are not colored, they simply evoke the sensation of color when processed by our nervous systems. Electromagnetic radiation with a wavelength of 495 nanometers is not cyan in color, of course, but it usually evokes the sensation of cyan in a color-normal observer.

Light falling on the retina may also vary in its spectral purity. It may not be made up of a single wavelength (indeed, it seldom is outside the laboratory) but many. This physical attribute of purity is related to the psychological, or perceived, quality of *saturation*. Thus, if we add white light (which is a very impure mixture of all the wavelengths in the visible spectrum) to, say, pure 490-nanometer light that is perceived as green, it appears to wash out and to become *desaturated* or whiter—a pastel green. Thus, another way of thinking of this purity (which gives rise to the impression of saturation or purity) is in terms of the amount of achromatic light added to monochromatic light. **Interaction 3.2.2**, in particular, is intended to give you a clear impression of what happens perceptually as saturation is continuously varied.

So, light waves can vary in wavelength, amplitude, and purity; and this usually gives rise to variations in perceived hue, brightness, and saturation. We can discriminate about 200 hues, 500 brightness values, and about 20 values of saturation, so this means we can discriminate about 2 million different colors (200 x 500 x 20). **Interaction 3.2.4**, which allows you to vary hue, saturation, and brightness independently, is designed to give you a good feel for how these three dimensions codetermine the perceptual quality of color. Be sure you understand, for instance, why you see only achromatic blacks and whites at extremes of brightness, whatever the hue and saturation chosen.

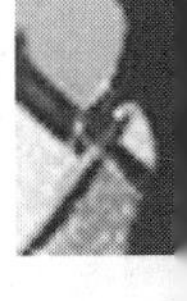

It is usual to organize and represent monochromatic hues (and some nonspectral colors) as a color wheel, an arrangement first proposed by Isaac Newton in 1704. The color wheel (or circle) derives from the fact that if colors are subjectively arranged by an observer—such that the most similar hues are arranged near each other—the resulting subjective arrangement, or structure, is not linear, but *circular*. You have the opportunity to assess this for yourself in **Interaction 3.2.1**, where you get to arrange colors in terms of their similarity. You should see quickly how necessary the circular arrangement of the colors is to a satisfying solution.

Note that the colors appear in the same order in the color wheel as they do in the color spectrum, and that complementary colors (red and green/blue and yellow) lie opposite each other on the color wheel. We return to these four colors again and again throughout this module; their relationships are of considerable theoretical importance. As noted, not all of the hues in the color wheel are monochromatic—that is, pure spectral colors. No single wavelength produces the impression of purple, which is a mixture of red and blue, or even red. And, as also noted, so-called unique red—that is, a red without a tinge of yellow or, indeed, any other color—is only observed when a tiny amount of blue is added to spectral red.

It is usual for the radius of the color circle to represent the dimension of saturation, with fully saturated colors at the circumference, or rim, and fully desaturated colors at the center, or hub, of the circle. The dimension of brightness, on which all the achromatic colors lie (white, grays, and black) can be thought of as running through the center of the circle, perpendicular to it—yielding a three-dimensional color solid or color spindle with white at the top and black at the base. We can think of all visible wavelengths as points in this color spindle. You can build this model yourself in **Interaction 3.2.5**.

The tapering, biconical shape of the spindle illustrates the fact that saturation is maximal only at moderate levels of brightness. The farther a hue is from the center of the brightness axis, the less its saturation. In this sense, very bright colors appear to be "washed out, " or desaturated. In the same way, when brightness is low, the impression of hue is again diminished. Colors appear muddy, weak, or desaturated. In this sense, saturation relates not only to spectral purity; it has a secondary dependence on brightness. In **Interaction 3.2.6** you can see which color results from any defined combination of hue, saturation, and brightness values. When you select a value on each of the three dimensions, you are, in effect, defining the locus of a color in the 3-D (spindle) color space. You will find this interaction particularly useful for exploring the implications of extremes of brightness for the perception of colors.

So, how does the color wheel, or color circle, relate to the color spindle? The color spindle can be thought of as a perpendicular stack of the color wheels associated with a particular brightness. Those color wheels progressively shrink—ultimately to a single point—at extremes of brightness. At those points, there exists only hueless white (where brightness is maximal) and hueless, or achromatic, black (where brightness is minimal).

If we take a horizontal slice through the spindle at the midpoint of the brightness axis, the result is the standard color circle. Wavelengths with their corresponding hues lie on the circumference of this circle. Degrees of saturation are represented along its radius, from 0% saturation at the hub or center of the circle to 100% saturation at its rim or circumference.

At the heart—the vertical core—of the color spindle is, then, an achromatic region of totally desaturated grays, including black and white. Fully saturated colors are never seen at high and low levels of brightness.

In effect, the color spindle summarizes, simplifies, and visually represents the relationships between the psychological dimensions of hue, saturation, and brightness.

Unit 3.3 Physiology of Color Vision

3.3.1 Types of Cones
3.3.2 Individual Cone Response Profiles
3.3.3 Cone Response Profiles and Hue

Humankind has long been beguiled by the question of how color vision arises. Any satisfying answer will require an understanding of the physical stimulus, the physiology of the visual system, and the subjective psychological world of the observer. In this unit, we focus on the physiological bases for color vision. The trichromatic and opponent process theories of color vision are examined in Units 3.5 and 3.6. Here, we focus on the physiological foundations upon which they are built: cone-pigment specialization in the retina and the identification of opponent processes higher in the visual system.

Of the two kinds of photoreceptors present in the retina—the rods and cones—only the latter appear to be implicated in color vision. Under minimal-illumination (scotopic) viewing conditions, when only the rods are active, there is no evidence for color vision.

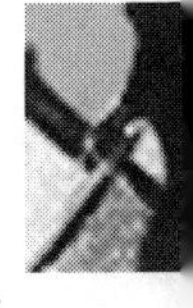

The history of our understanding of color vision provides a nice example of how psychological data—in particular, evidence from the psychophysics of color matching—can provide insights into the likely nature of the underlying physiology.

Almost 200 years ago, Thomas Young (1773–1829) proposed a three-receptor theory of color vision, which was developed, in 1866, by Hermann von Helmholtz (1821–1894) into a fully articulated trichromatic theory in which each receptor, in effect, had different spectral sensitivities.

At the heart of this theory was the proposition that all color sensations were produced by the proportional, integrated contributions of these three receptors. Across-fiber pattern coding (see Unit 1.8) has very deep historical roots indeed. It was proposed that each receptor type (cone) contained a distinctive pigment, each bleached by light of a different wavelength. These were identified as *erythrolabe* ("red-catching"), *chlorolabe* ("green-catching"), and *cyanolabe* ("blue-catching") pigments, largely on the basis of psychophysical, color-matching evidence. Helmholtz went so far as to propose hypothetical excitation curves for these three classes of receptors and used them to make quantitative predictions about the ability of humans to discriminate colors.

It was another 100 years before detailed physiological evidence emerged for three cone groups, or types, each containing a specialized pigment, which maximally bleaches in the presence of light of particular wavelengths to yield a distinctive electrochemical response. The first direct physiological evidence for three specialized cone pigments came from a series of *microspectrophotometry* studies in the mid-1960s (for example, Brown & Wald, 1964; Marks, Dobelle, & MacNichol, 1964). In essence, this technique involves shining tightly focused monochromatic light on the pigment-bearing part of the cone and carefully recording the amount of light absorbed by the pigment as a function of the wavelength of that light. The result was relative absorption spectra for each of the three cone types. These data provided, in effect, a firm physiological foundation for the trichromacy of human vision.

Thus, three classes of cones were identified in this way, each absorbing light across a range of wavelengths, but maximally sensitive to light of a particular, distinctive wavelength. **Interaction 3.3.1** epitomizes this "tuned" spectral sensitivity of each cone type. In general terms, the three cone types appeared to be tuned to absorb light of short (S), medium (M), and long (L) wavelengths, being maximally responsive in the human eye to 435-nm, 535-nm, and 565-nm light, respectively (Brown & Wald, 1964; but see also Bowmaker & Dartnell, 1980, who suggest peak absorbance at 419-nm, 531-nm and 558-nm, for S, M, and L cones, respectively). These cone types are sometimes referred to (much too loosely) as blue, green, and red cones, respectively, but (strictly) they peak in the violet, yellow-green, and orange regions of the color spectrum. Here, we refer to them simply as S, M, and L cones. For convenience, the cone types are color-coded in the various interactions in this module—but take care not to interpret this coding too literally.

The most fascinating question, here, is how can three receptor types uniquely code the approximately 200 hues that humans can distinguish? The answer appears to lie in the fact that, at each wavelength, the activity, or responsiveness, profile of the three cone types is slightly different. It is important that you grasp how color might be powerfully coded in this way, and **Interactions 3.3.3** and **3.3.4** should help you do this. Interaction 3.3.3 displays the cone-response profile for each wavelength in the spectrum of visible light. Interaction 3.3.4 maps those response profiles to the specific hues in the conventional color wheel model.

Interactions 3.3.5 and **3.3.6** illustrate a similar phenomenon in all three cone types. Each of the cone types is "tuned" to respond maximally to light of a particular wavelength, but it is possible to get a similar response to a light stimulus of nonoptimal wavelength if the intensity of the stimulus is increased. It is not spelled out in those interactions, but nonetheless important, that increasing light intensity will elevate the response of a given cone type to light of all the wavelengths to which it is sensitive.

You can think of the consequences of increasing intensity as displacing the entire response curve up the *Response* axis (see Goldstein,

1996, Figure 4.8). Thus, a particular response from a particular cone receptor does not signal a specific wavelength—a vital consideration in color coding. So, a response of (say) 15 may characterize (be indicative of) one wavelength at a low intensity and an entirely different wavelength at a higher stimulus intensity. In the same way, at any given intensity, a cone receptor can respond identically to light of more than one wavelength. Thus, the response level in any one cone cannot unambiguously signal stimulation by light of a given wavelength.

These observations are important for the commentary they provide on the neural coding of sensory qualities, a topic dealt with in several interactions in Module 1. Because any one cone cannot unambiguously signal stimulation by light of a given wavelength, labeled-lines coding of color is ruled out. Across-fiber coding must be implicated. This feature ties Interactions 3.3.5 and 3.3.6 back into Interactions 3.3.2 and 3.3.3: it is clearly the pattern of response in the three cone types—the response profile of the S, M, and L cones—that is the basis of the code for color, not the activity of any one cone type.

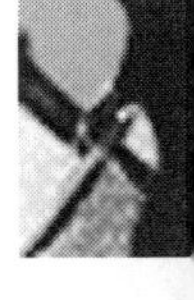

Because neither the cones in general, nor the particular classes of cones, are uniformly distributed across the retina, the color response varies from region to region. Cones are densely packed in the central fovea, for instance, but that region is relatively insensitive to blue. In the same way, the ability to see green diminishes as a function of angular distance from the fovea. Why might this be? In general terms, color vision disappears in the order green, red, yellow, and blue as we move from the fovea to the periphery.

If any, or all, of the three cone pigments is missing, human color vision will be deficient in predictable ways. You can explore these color-vision deficits in detail in Unit 3.7.

Unit 3.4 Color Mixing

3.4.1 Additive Color Mixing
3.4.2 Subtractive Color Mixing
3.4.3 Subtractive Mixing with Pigments
3.4.4 Color Mixing and Saturation
3.4.5 Mixing Complementary Colors
3.4.6 Mixing Primary Colors

We seldom see pure hues outside the laboratory. Usually, the light reaching the eye is a mixture of wavelengths. Generally, the dominant wavelength tends to determine the perceived hue—but that is not always the case. Under certain conditions, when two or more lights of different wavelength are combined, a new hue is perceived. The mixing of lights of different wavelength is termed *additive* because all the component wavelengths reach the retina, where their excitations are summed. This is usually contrasted with *subtractive mixing*, which occurs when light-absorbing pigments, rather than lights, are mixed. When white light falls on the mixed pigments, certain parts of the spectrum—certain wavelengths—are subtracted, or absorbed. The light energy reflected to the eye is less than that falling on the mixture, and its spectral composition is different.

Consider what happens when white light falls on a mixture of blue and yellow pigments, as is the case in **Interaction 3.4.3**. The blue pigment absorbs the wavelengths corresponding to red, orange, and yellow and reflects the short wavelengths corresponding to violet, blue, and green. On the other hand, the yellow pigment absorbs those violet-blue wavelengths. This leaves only the wavelengths corresponding to green—the rest have been subtracted from the white light falling on the blue-yellow mix. So, when blue and green pigments are subtractively mixed, the perceptual result is green. In this sense, pigments can be thought of as comprising tiny filters tuned to absorb light of certain wavelengths.

Lights, on the other hand, combine additively. All of the wavelengths of light being combined actually arrive at the photoreceptors, rather than being filtered, or subtracted out, beforehand. The light energy of the mixture is the additive sum of the energies of the component wavelengths. The mixing (addition) takes place in the visual system; the effects of the component visual excitations, or visual effects, add. Once additively mixed by the eye, lights of different color cannot subsequently be analyzed or teased apart.

The color circle is particularly useful in allowing us to predict the results of mixing light of different wavelength, and you should note carefully this feature of the interactions in this unit.

So, what if one mixes blue and yellow lights, rather than pigments? The result is achromatic gray. The blue light—with its shorter wavelengths corresponding to violet blue, and green—adds to the yellow light, with its longer wavelength elements of yellow, red, and orange. The result is a mixture of lights across the whole spectrum of visible light—perceived as achromatic gray.

Blue and yellow are, of course, complementary colors and mixing any two complementary colors in equal proportions results in gray. Complementary colors lie directly opposite each other in the color circle, literally diametrically opposed. This general principle is illustrated in **Interaction 3.4.5**, where you have the opportunity to mix blue and yellow, then red and green.

To be more accurate, this latter complementary pair is (strictly) red and blue-green. Similarly, if you inspect the color circle carefully, you will notice that green and *purple* are complementary, lying directly opposite each other. You may remember that purple is a *nonspectral*, or *extraspectral*, color; it is not monochromatic, but a mix of spectral red and blue lights. This is a case, then, where the complement of a spectral color (green) is not itself a spectral color (purple).

You should keep these principles regarding complementary colors in mind as you work through the various interactions in this module, particularly those dealing with color aftereffects. **Interaction 3.4.4** allows you to carefully explore what happens when noncomplementary colors of light are mixed in various proportions. Interaction 3.4.4 is effectively a working model of color mixing based on the color circle. A critical point to note is that all color mixes are more or less desaturated. In a two-color mix, the resultant color is always less saturated than one, or both, of its constituents. Be sure you understand why. You should also be able to work out from Interaction 3.4.4 a general principle regarding the mixing of colors: Will they be more or less saturated the farther they are away from each other on the color wheel?

As noted, once spectral lights are combined, an observer cannot split them apart or analyze the light into its component wavelengths (or hues). With respect to mixtures, vision is a synthetic, rather than analytic, sense. It can be contrasted with, say, taste and audition—which are analytic senses: we can hear both the cellos and the trumpets simultaneously at a symphony concert, and taste both the vinegar and the pepper in a salad dressing.

It is important to note that additive mixing does not change the lights in any way, only our perception of them. In this sense, the consequences of additive mixing are subjective and perceptual, not external and physical. Also observe that two chromatic surfaces may have dramatically different spectral compositions (be composed of dramatically different combinations of wavelengths of light) yet appear identical. Such colors are called *metameric colors* or simply *metamers*. Thus, a mixture of red and green light can reproduce the color sensation evoked by a monochromatic spectral yellow light. These two yellows (having a different spectral composition, but appearing identical because their impacts on the visual system are identical) are metamers. They constitute a *metameric pair*.

Not all of painting with pigments involves subtractive color mixing. The technique called *pointillism*, which involves placing myriad, tiny, discrete dots of paint of different hue in close proximity, involves additive mixing. When viewed from a distance, the colors merge and mix to yield new hues and take on a luminous quality. We see examples of pointillism in the work of Georges Seurat and others of the French impressionist school of painting. Precisely the same pointillist principle, where the eye blends and mixes the colors, is used in color television. Tiny red, green, and blue dots—too small to be discriminated at normal viewing distances—are combined by the eye to yield all the colors of the rainbow, and more. Many tapestries and intricate embroideries utilize the same pointillist principles and the powerful additive mixing of lights of different colors by the visual system.

A basic tenet of trichromatic theory is that one can match any color by mixing light of any three primary colors. Lights that appear roughly green, blue, and red are often used as primaries, but many different sets of colors can be used in this way. There are two constraints, however: none of the set should be able to be matched by a mixture of the other two; and no two of the primaries can be complementary colors. When mixed in equal proportions, a set of primary colored lights will yield white light, but by adjusting the *proportion* of each light in the mixture it is possible to match any monochromatic color. Remember that the color resulting from the mixture and the monochromatic standard color are metamers.

You can check how this works in **Interaction 3.4.6**, where the task (for convenience) is to match the color of two tulips. Monochromatic tulips never occur in Nature! In actual color-matching experiments, an observer views two adjacent white surfaces as a split field. One (the standard) is illuminated by a monochromatic light source and the other (the comparison surface) by the three primary-color light sources. The observer mixes the latter until the perceived hues of the standard and comparison surfaces are the same. If this matching procedure is repeated for monochromatic standard light sources right across the spectrum, the result is color-mixture curves like those shown in Interaction 3.4.6. The spectral compositions of the light coming from the standard and the comparison stimuli are radically different: their apparent equivalence is entirely psychological.

An unusual feature of the color-mixture curves in Interaction 3.4.6 is the fact that the amount of a color in the mixture is occasionally *negative*. What this means in physical terms is that, to achieve a match, it is sometimes necessary to add a little light of one color to the "wrong" side of the split field: the light of one or more of the primary colors is added to the monochromatic standard, thereby desaturating it.

This means that we must add an important caveat to our general proposition regarding color mixing, as exemplified in Interaction 3.4.6. We cannot (strictly) match light of any color using light of any three primary colors. What we can do is achieve a metameric match of two colors using three primaries, *but only if negative amounts of one or more primaries can be used.* Thus, the two sides of the split field can be made to look identical, but only if one can add the three primary colors to either half-field.

Unit 3.5 Opponent Process Theory

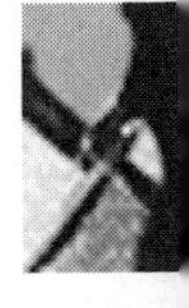

Data from experiments on color afterimages, simultaneous color contrast, color naming, color-vision deficits, and complementary colors pose difficulties for an unelaborated trichromatic theory of color vision. Some of these problems have been apparent for over 100 years. As early as 1878, Ewald Hering spelled out the need for an alternative account of color vision, the essence of which is now called *opponent process theory.* It seemed to Hering that humans behaved as if there were four primary colors (red, green, blue, and yellow), not three and, if that were the case, any trichromatic color theory was necessarily mistaken.

In the psychophysics of color experience, it appears that blue and yellow and red and green are mutually exclusive. An object may appear green or red, but not both at the same time, just as an object may appear blue or yellow, but not both at the same time. We do not see reddish greens or bluish yellows, even though we see reddish yellows and bluish greens. Hering was the first to posit—on the basis of a range of phenomenological observations—that the visual system may treat red-green and blue-yellow as antagonistic, or opponent, pairs. He suggested there were neural "substances," which accounted for observed red-green opposition, blue-yellow opposition, and achromatic black-white opposition.

These substances were held by Hering to respond positively to stimulation by one color in each pair and negatively to the other. In this way, they potentially could "signal" the presence of one color in each pair, but not both. The achromatic black-white substance was deemed to respond negatively to the former and positively to the latter, whereas the chromatic red-green substance responded positively to red stimulation and negatively to green. Finally, the response to blue was held to be negative, whereas that to yellow was deemed positive.

In this module of *Exploring Perception*, we concentrate on the opponency of chromatic colors, but you should bear in mind that the same general principles apply to the achromatic colors black and white.

Recent proponents of this view have referred to opponent *processes* or *channels* rather than *substances*. The term *channel* has a specialized meaning in perception, usually denoting a set of nerve fibers carrying, or relaying, a common, shared message. Hering found support for this theory in his observations of color-vision deficits. Those color-blind to red do not see green either, and those color-blind to blue do not see yellow. The precise nature of color-vision deficits is explored in detail in Unit 3.7. They are germane, here, to the extent that they provide good evidence for the opponent process model of color vision.

Hering suggested that the physiological basis for opponent process theory was substances, or chemicals, in the retina, which built up and broke down depending on the nature of the light falling on them. Although there is no evidence for such retinal substances (and Hering was certainly incorrect regarding the physiological substrate of his elegant theory), there is good evidence for neurons in the visual systems of primates and infraprimate species that respond to stimulation by light of different wavelengths in ways broadly consistent with Hering's opponency principles.

In general terms, these cells—found in the retina, the lateral geniculate nucleus and the cortex of various species—are excited by light of a band of wavelengths toward one end of the electromagnetic spectrum and inhibited by a band of wavelengths toward the other end (for example, Svaetichin, 1956; Svaetichin & MacNichol, 1958; Devalois & DeValois, 1980; Devalois & Jacobs, 1984; Derrington, Lennie, & Krauskopf, 1983; Hubel & Livingstone, 1990) . *Excitation* means that the cell's firing rate *increases* from some baseline rate, and *inhibition* connotes a *decrease* in the firing rate.

Study **Interaction 3.5.1** in some detail. The principles embodied in red-green opponent-cell operation are both straightforward and general. If you clearly understand what is happening in Interaction 3.5.1, then you should have little trouble with the (sometimes challenging) material in the remainder of this module.

Note that, although retinal events (related to the cones and other retinal cells) may help shape the experience of color, the actual perception of color does not occur until much higher in the visual system. It is clear that simultaneous color contrast, color cancellation, and color aftereffects, for example, are higher-level, opponent-cell phenomena.

The color-canceling paradigm simulated in **Interaction 3.5.2** is important, not only for the commentary it provides on opponent processing, but because it epitomizes the logic of the methodology used by Hurvich and Jameson to derive the relative-strength curves at the heart of **Interactions 3.5.3** and **3.5.4**. In essence, they established the relative strength of the color mechanisms across the spectrum by determining how much of an opponent color was necessary to cancel the targeted color impression.

It will become clear, as you work through later units in this module, that trichromatic theory and opponent process theory are in fact complementary. Trichromatic theory does a good job of describing color coding at the retinal level, whereas opponent process theory appears to capture the nature of color processing higher in the visual system. It might seem that such an arrangement is rather redundant, or inelegant. Why have two color-coding systems when one should probably suffice? Somewhat surprisingly, the outputs from the three cone types (because their absorption spectra substantially overlap) are highly correlated, hence somewhat redundant. This is particularly the case for the M and L cones, as you probably will have noticed in Unit 3.3. The nervous system is not usually so wasteful. But, as Buchsbaum and Gottschalk (1983) have demonstrated statistically, a system in which output from three cone types is fed to three opponent cell types before being relayed to the brain may be an exceedingly efficient way of maximizing the transmission of color. You might find their work interesting to follow up. You will find a handy introduction to it in Sekuler and Blake (1994, pp. 205–206). Unit 3.6 looks in more detail at how the integration of these two theories (trichromatic theory and opponent process theory) might be accomplished.

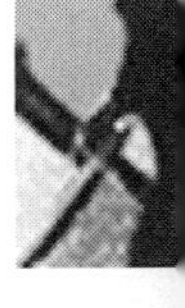

Unit 3.6 Synthesizing Theories of Color Vision

3.6.1 Adding Yellow Light to Blue
3.6.2 Problems for Trichromacy Alone
3.6.3 Afterimages and Red-Green Opponent Cells
3.6.4 Afterimages and Blue-Yellow Opponent Cells

3.6.5 Opponency or Trichromacy?
3.6.6 How Colors Are Coded

This unit examines some phenomena that pose a problem for any unelaborated trichromatic theory of color vision (Interactions 3.6.1 and 3.6.2) and shows how these might be accommodated by the opponent process model (Interactions 3.6.3 and 3.6.4). Finally, it shows how these two theories might be integrated into a single, hybrid theory in which trichromatic retinal operations feed into opponent processes higher in the visual system (Interactions 3.6.5 and 3.6.6).

Interaction 3.6.1 provides a simulation similar in logic to that in Interaction 3.5.2, where the blue component of extraspectral violet light is canceled by the addition of yellow light. The perception of extraspectral violet implies (in opponent process terms) output from both the red-green opponent cell (signaling red) and the blue-yellow cell (signaling blue). As yellow light is added and the firing rate of the blue-yellow opponent cell returns to baseline (neither blue nor yellow is signaled), the resulting red light reflects the output of the red-green opponent cell alone.

In Interaction 3.6.1, cancellation is not of one color from a color mixture, but of one color (blue) by its complement (yellow). Stimulated by blue light, the activity of the blue-yellow cell is depressed below baseline, due to inhibitory input from the S cones. Progressive addition of yellow light returns the activity of the cell to baseline and the perception of achromatic gray. In this sense, adding yellow *diminishes* the blue response of the blue-yellow opponent cell. Yellow's excitatory input—via summation of M- and L-cone excitatory responses—progressively nullifies the inhibitory input of the S cones, and the cell's firing rate increases until it approaches baseline. In effect, the blue response is *neutralized* or *nullified* by the yellow light. The blue-yellow opponent cell can signal blue *or* yellow, but *it cannot signal both.*

It is important to note that this cancellation paradigm is simply a special case of the additive mixing of complementary colors explored in Interaction 3.4.5. Remember, when complementary colors—whether spectral or extraspectral—are additively mixed in equal proportions, the result is always an achromatic gray. So, color cancellation is achieved in Interaction 3.6.1 by, in effect, additively mixing complementary colors.

Trichromatic theory provides no adequate explanation of why complementary colors mix to give achromatic gray. Similarly, complementary color aftereffects of the kind examined in **Interaction 3.6.2** pose a problem for trichromatic theory. Opponent process theory, in contrast, provides a satisfying account of the complementary color aftereffects experienced after prolonged exposure to light of a given wavelength. You can explore these explanations in detail through the simulations in **Interactions 3.6.3** and **3.6.4**. The explanatory principles underpinning both interactions are precisely the same. They will take a little time to complete, but if you fully understand these interactions, you will be well on the way to understanding the opponent process theory of color vision.

Interaction 3.6.5 integrates trichromatic and opponent process theories of color vision in a simple simulation. Each of the cones responds to part of the spectrum of electromagnetic energy and, as you saw in Interaction 3.2.1 fires maximally to a specific wavelength. Output from the cones feeds to the blue-yellow and red-green opponent cells. Input from the photoreceptors either excites (+) or inhibits (–) firing of the opponent cell. The blue-yellow cell gets inhibitory input from the S cone proportional to its spectral sensitivity/responsivity, and summed excitatory input from the M and L cones.

The R-G cell gets excitatory input from the L cone and inhibitory input from the M cone. In both cases, input from the cones is, again, proportional to their responsivity to light of various wavelengths. In this system, it is assumed that trichromatic theory adequately describes retinal/photoreceptor functioning, and that opponent process theory provides a good description of color coding higher in the visual system (for example, the lateral geniculate nucleus and the cortex).

Interaction 3.6.6 shows how color may be coded by making use of the distinctive response profiles of the cones at each wavelength and the summation-distillation of their output by the opponent cells operating in tandem. The system is simple, but powerful, and you probably will find it useful to spend some time ensuring that you understand this simulation of the two color theories and, in particular, how it is that they conjointly can code (signal) stimulation of the system by light of a particular wavelength.

Unit 3.7 Pathologies of Color Vision

There is a wide range of "normal" variation in human color vision. The variations tend to be subtle and usually without functional significance in everyday life. A very small percentage of people, however, show what might be termed pathologies of color vision.

Trichromatic color vision predicts five classes of color vision abnormality, all of which can be explored in this unit. Only one of those can properly be termed color *blindness*: monochromats have no functioning cones and see a world of black, white, and shades of gray. They are sometimes called *rod monochromats*, because only their rods are fully functional. In general terms, monochromats have poor visual acuity and find daylight (photopic) viewing uncomfortable.

The remaining four varieties of color deficiency can be readily understood in terms of which of the three cone types is nonfunctional (usually caused by an absence of the specialized pigments that characterize them). If only one cone type is operational in addition to the rods, color discrimination is still impossible. In other words, individuals with no functioning cones, and those with only one active cone type, see the world in much the same way: all colors are seen simply as gradations of intensity or lightness (white, gray, and black). This constitutes a second class of monochromatism. Monochromats can match any wavelength in the visible spectrum by simply adjusting the intensity of any other wavelength.

Individuals with only one cone type nonfunctional, having two cone types operating normally, are termed *dichromats.* They have some color discrimination, but it is quite different from normal color vision. The precise kind of deficit depends on which of the three cone types is nonfunctional: those maximally sensitive to short (S), medium (M), or long (L) wavelength light.

Individuals with nonfunctioning L cones are termed *protanopes*, those with defective M cones are termed *deuteranopes*, and those with abnormal S cones are called *tritanopes.* A dichromat needs only two wavelengths to match all other wavelengths of light in the visible spectrum. Loss of either the M- or L-cones results in the red-green channel being eliminated, but the blue-yellow channel remains functional, albeit in a modified form. In the rare cases where the S cones are nonfunctional, the blue-yellow chromatic channel is lost, leaving only the red-green channel operative.

Protanopes are insensitive to long wavelength light in the orange-red range and tend to report wavelengths above 492 nm as yellow and wavelengths below 492 nm as blue (see **Interactions 3.7.2** and **3.7.5**). Similarly, deuteranopes are insensitive to medium wavelength light in the green range. Again, they tend to report wavelengths above 498 nm as yellow and wavelengths below 498 nm as blue. Somewhat paradoxically, tritanopes, who have defective color vision in the short-wavelength blue-violet range, do not report short wavelengths (< 570 nm) as green, but as *blue*. They see the longer wavelengths correctly as red.

Thus, the perceived color spectra of dichromats are differentiated into two regions: shorter wavelengths tend to be seen as one color (blue) and longer wavelengths as another (either yellow, in the case of protanopes and deuteranopes, or red in the case of tritanopes). All three classes of dichromat have *neutral points* in their seen color spectrum, that is, wavelengths (spectral locations) that are perceived as gray. Those neutral points occur at the boundaries between the two regions. In all three classes of dichromatism, the seen color tends to desaturate at wavelengths approaching the neutral point.

It is important to note that the physiological bases of monochromatism and dichromatism are different: monochromats usually have no cones, or only one of the three cone types present, whereas dichromatism is due to the absence of one of the three visual pigments. Thus, in the case of dichromats, all three cone types are present but one is nonfunctional because of the absence of a critical pigment.

There is also a class of *anomalous trichromats*, who—like normal trichromats—need three wavelengths to match any given wavelength. Anomalous trichromats will mix those wavelengths in different proportions from normals, however, probably because of abnormal absorption by their pigments. Thus, color matches that satisfy anomalous trichromats will not look correct to normal trichromats. Unlike dichromats, anomalous trichromats have no neutral point.

There are also a few *unilateral dichromats* in the population. This group is particularly interesting because they enable us to establish precisely what colors dichromats see. Unilateral dichromats have one dichromatic eye and one normal trichromatic eye. Thus, they are able to report which color in the dichromatic eye corresponds to a given color in the trichromatic eye.

There is some interesting variation in the frequency of color-vision deficits in males in various populations. About 8% of Caucasian males show deficits, 5% of Asian males, and 3% of African-American and Native-American males. The incidence of color-vision deficits is strikingly higher in males than in females (about ten times greater in the case of Caucasians). Recent evidence suggests that some females may indeed have supernormal color vision with four-pigment (*tetrachromatic*) color vision.

It is important to note that, because color and lightness typically covary, people with color-vision deficits can sometimes distinguish between two colors on the basis of differences in lightness. For this reason, tests of color vision (such as the ubiquitous Ishihara plates most often used) must take great care to equate lightness in order to provide no clue to color. If this were not done in the case of the Ishihara plates, it could be possible to read the embedded dot-defined numerals because of differences in lightness; someone with deficient color vision might perform quite well.

Unit 3.8 Afterimages and Simultaneous Color Contrast

3.8.1 Complementary Color Afterimages
3.8.2 "Oh, say can you see . . . "
3.8.3 Other Flag Afterimages
3.8.4 Afterimages the Easy Way
3.8.5 Simultaneous Color Contrast
3.8.6 The McCollough Effect

Prolonged exposure to light of a given wavelength, or hue, can result in a negative or complementary color afterimage. This simple phenomenon has important implications for theories of color vision, as was noted in Unit 3.6. In particular, color aftereffects pose difficulties for any unelaborated trichromatic theory of color perception, whereas they are well explained by opponent process theory.

Interaction 3.6.3 provides you with the opportunity to simulate the process of color adaptation, and consequent aftereffect, in the red-green opponent cell. Interaction 3.6.4 provides an analogous simulation for the blue-yellow opponent cell. A clear understanding of the process and principles at work in those two interactions will provide you with a sound basis for understanding and interpreting the range of phenomena presented in this final unit of Module 3.

Unit 3.8 also illustrates a second phenomenon, which is at odds with trichromatic theory: *simultaneous color contrast.* Color contrast (the situation in which the appearance of one color surrounded by another is changed by the surrounding color) is one of a range of spatial interactions common in the visual system. In this sense, the color contrast demonstration in Interaction 3.8.5 is conceptually related to, for instance, simultaneous brightness contrast (Interaction 4.8.4); the phenomenon of Mach bands (Interaction 4.6.3); and lateral inhibition generally (Interactions 1.5.1 and 1.5.2). Indeed, it is highly likely that simultaneous brightness contrast, Mach bands, and color contrast arise from the action of similar mechanisms—varieties of lateral inhibition. If this is so, it should be possible, for instance, to generate the equivalent of Mach bands in grating stimuli that vary in color rather than in brightness, and there is some evidence that this is the case (Ware & Cowan, 1987).

Color contrast is a powerful phenomenon often encountered outside the laboratory, but it can require something of a keen and analytical observational sense—a "trained" eye. You have probably encountered it with clothing: the appearance of (say) a white shirt, or blouse, appears to vary depending on the color of the sweater, or jacket, you wear with it. A red sweater may lend a blue-green tinge to the shirt, whereas a green jacket will lend a red tinge. These colors are spatially induced by their complementary colors. Put simply, colors are affected by the color of adjacent objects.

Simultaneous color contrast is not always an unwanted by-product; artists often use it deliberately to achieve unusual effects. Sekuler and Blake (1994, Box 6.3, pp. 202–203) provide an interesting account of the use of simultaneous color contrast by, for example, Paul Chevreul in the Gobelin tapestries and by Edwin Land, inventor of the Polaroid camera. The French Impressionists made considerable use of Chevreul's principles regarding color harmony and contrast.

Interesting interactive color effects also may be obtained when one's gaze is shifted to a neutral, or colored, surface after prolonged exposure to another color—the phenomenon of successive color contrast. If gaze is shifted to a gray or white surface, it will take on the hue of the inducing color's complement. This is usually described as a complementary afterimage, rather than as a special case of successive color contrast. If gaze is shifted to a colored surface, the colors of afterimage and surface merge, yielding a unitary, or fused, color sensation, not decomposable into its constituents. The results can be startling. When gaze is shifted to a green surface after prolonged exposure to red, the result can be a supersaturated "greener-than-green." The greens of the afterimage and the surface appear to sum.

The necessary precursor to generating a color afterimage is prolonged exposure to a color stimulus (say, red), during which the retinal photoreceptors sensitive to red become fatigued. The color response is diminished as adaptation runs its course; a red inspection patch will appear to fade, or become desaturated, as fatigue takes hold. This fading, or desaturation, is very obvious during the inspection period—try it and see!

The simulation in Interaction 3.6.3 tracks this adaptation process. As is clear from that interaction, prolonged exposure to red is functionally equivalent to increasing the system's sensitivity to green. When stimulation by red is ceased, a green afterimage results: in terms of the

Interaction 3.6.3 model, the inhibitory M-cone input is no longer balanced by excitatory input from the L-cone (because of its fatigued state) and the red-green opponent cell's firing rate is below baseline—signaling green.

It is possible to explain simultaneous color contrast as a special, local case of this kind of negative aftereffect. In terms of the earlier example of simultaneous color contrast, the red receptors are fatigued during fixation on the red jacket and it loses saturation. Momentary deflection of gaze to the white blouse means the M cone's inhibitory input to the opponent cell exceeds the (fatigued) L cone's excitatory input. Thus, the cell signals green when gaze is directed at the white blouse.

Notice in the several examples of negative afterimages, available in **Interactions 3.8.1** to **3.8.4**, that those afterimages are considerably less saturated than the inducing colors. This is due, in part, to *fusing* of the afterimage color with the achromatic white/gray of the screen against which the afterimage is viewed. As noted earlier, if the afterimages were viewed against a surface or screen of *similar* color, color fusion would make the surface appear *supersaturated.*

Clearly, simultaneous and successive color contrast and negative afterimages are intimately related phenomena. They neatly exemplify the power of the hybrid trichromatic–opponent process theory simulated in Interactions 3.6.5 and 3.6.6.

Within this context, the McCollough effect examined in the final interaction in this module (**Interaction 3.8.6**), is disconcerting. In the McCollough effect, prolonged exposure to (say) a red-black vertical grating and a green-black horizontal grating results in *orientation specific* negative aftereffects when observers, subsequently, are presented with a black-and-white grating. All of the aftereffect and contrast effects dealt with in this unit are transitory, almost fleeting. As such, they are neatly dealt with in terms of localized receptor fatigue and recovery. The McCollough effect, however, is disconcertingly long-lasting. It can last weeks in some cases! Sensory effects are typically much more transient. Clearly, the McCollough effect is not retinal, sensory, or peripheral in nature, but occurs much higher in the visual system. Murch (1976) has suggested that the effect is caused by a form of classical conditioning, but this account begs more questions than it answers. Why, for instance, are other apparently peripheral sensory events not similarly conditioned?

Module 4

Depth, Size, Brightness, and Contrast

Unit 4.1 Cues to Depth

A striking feature of human perception is that we effortlessly perceive depth, seeing the world in three spatial dimensions despite having only two 2-dimensional representations of it in the retinal images. Clearly, there are many features, or cues, in those retinal images that map directly onto physical differences in depth in the viewed world. If the outline of an object A is partly obscured by object B, for example, we can conclude that the latter is closer. If we know those two objects are of equal size, then the object whose image-size on the retina is smaller must be more distant.

It seems that we learn the relationships between those cues and depth in the field of view and, having done that, utilize them (effortlessly and automatically) to make assumptions about the relative location of objects in three-dimensional space. A vast range of human activities require detailed, accurate information about the spatial relationships between objects and surfaces in the environment and ourselves. It may be the very automaticity of depth perception that is responsible for the many depth-related illusions we experience.

It is usual, and convenient, to classify depth cues as being of four types: pictorial, oculomotor, binocular disparity, and movement-produced cues. All are covered in some detail in this module. **Interactions 4.1.1** and **4.1.2** cover a range of pictorial cues to depth, including the interposition of objects, height in the field of view, familiar size, relative size, textural gradients, aerial perspective, and linear perspective. Shading, another powerful pictorial depth cue, is dealt with in **Interaction 4.1.3**.

Pictorial depth cues are so-called because they are the cues an artist might use in creating the impression of depth (three-dimensionality) in a painting, or drawing, on a flat (two-dimensional) surface. Pictorial cues are monocular, in the sense that only one eye is required to fully utilize them. Insofar as *all* depth cues in respect of *distant* objects are monocular, they are clearly of some significance.

All of the monocular depth cues dealt with in this unit are pictorial and *static* cues, in the sense that they require no movement of either object or observer to provide useful spatial information. You have the opportunity in Unit 4.5 to explore *movement-mediated* monocular depth cues, such as *motion parallax* (Interaction 4.5.1), the *kinetic depth effect* (Interaction 4.5.2), and *optical flow* (Interaction 4.5.3). All rely on movement of the observer and/or object to generate depth information.

There is a second kind of movement-produced (but *binocular*) depth cue called stereo-motion, which you can investigate in Interaction 4.5.4. Based on our ability to discriminate between the rates of change of location of the image of an object in the two retinal images, stereo-motion provides cues both to the relative depth of an object in the field of view and its direction of movement relative to the observer.

Not only do objects exist at some depth from an observer, but those objects have depth, or three-dimensional shape. In essence, shape consists in the relative disposition of the parts of an object in space. Solid, three-dimensional objects typically cast shadows. When light from a single source falls on such an object, it creates areas of light and dark: light falls directly on some areas, obliquely on others, and some areas are shaded from the light entirely. Typically, those areas closest to the light source receive the most illumination. Clearly, shading is a fundamental source of spatial information. It can be thought of as a perspective cue for this reason. Depth cues are provided, in effect, by the pattern of light and shading. That pattern will change, of course, as the direction of the light source changes relative to the object.

Shading is an interesting perceptual phenomenon, not only for its role as a static monocular depth cue, but because it exemplifies the constructive, top-down nature of much of perception. One's assumptions play a critical role in how the intensity gradients set up by shading are interpreted, and it is worth spending some time understanding the principles at work in Interaction 4.1.3 for precisely that reason.

In the absence of firm evidence to the contrary, most observers make the implicit assumption that the light source is *directly overhead* the viewed object. Stunning reversal can occur when a picture is rotated relative to the apparent light source, as it is in Interaction 4.1.3. In addition to assumptions about light source location, other implicit assumptions guide the way in which patterns of shading are interpreted. For instance, we tend to assume (for obvious reasons) that faces are *convex*, projecting outward. Shown the (*concave*) inside of a face mask, that assumption overrides our preconception about the location of light sources: there is a strong tendency, in this case, to see a conventional, convex face lit from below.

Other assumptions also appear to play an important role in the way we interpret the pattern of light and shade on a surface. There appears to be a bias toward observing shadowy surfaces as being far away from the light source. Highlighted surfaces are seen as being closer.

Apparent depth increases as *contrast* increases (Berbaum, Tharp, & Mroczek, 1983). Artists deliberately set up intensity gradients across a two-dimensional surface to create the impression of depth. This ruse works because of our wide, real-world experience of such gradients and the automaticity of so much of depth perception: because the surface of a flat plane does not throw shadows, observed shadows must be due to "three-dimensional objects" inscribed on that surface.

You can explore two powerful oculomotor cues to depth—*convergence* and *accommodation*—in **Interactions 4.1.4** and **4.1.5**, respectively. Both depend on our ability to utilize feedback from muscles in and around the eye to make inferences about the disposition of objects in space. In the case of convergence, information is sourced from the muscles that rotate the eyes so that a target object remains foveally fixated. They must be rotated inward (converged) to foveally fixate close objects and rotated outward (diverged) to fixate more distant objects. Thus, knowledge of the relative state of convergence of the eyes can be a valuable cue to depth.

Be sure you understand the reason why convergence is a useful cue to the relative depth of close, but not distant, objects. Interaction 4.1.4 should make that clear, if you carefully monitor the magnitude of *changes* in convergence angle as a function of depth in the field of view. Although accommodation is, clearly, a *monocular* depth cue (useful information about ciliary muscle pressure can be obtained from one eye), convergence is necessarily *binocular*.

Interaction 4.1.6 is based on the logic of a classic experiment, which demonstrated that observers actually used ocular convergence as a depth cue. The key point here is that because a potential cue—a detectable depth-indexing physical difference—*exists* does not entail that humans *utilize* it in practice.

Unit 4.2 Visual Angle, Retinal Size, and Distance

This unit is concerned with the important relationship between size and distance. In particular, the interactions in this unit are designed to give you: (i) a clear understanding of the notion of visual angle; (ii) an appreciation of how visual angle changes with viewing distance and the size of an object; (iii) enough information to allow you to calculate visual angle as the need arises; and (iv) an introduction to the principle of size-distance scaling, together with an indication of how it might be applied in estimating the likely size of afterimages.

By the end of this unit you should have no trouble explaining how objects of different size can subtend the same visual angle; how an object of fixed size can subtend an infinite number of visual angles; or how to calculate visual angle. As well as knowing how to calculate visual angle, hopefully you will have developed clear appreciation of why it is useful for a student of visual perception to be able to do so.

It will be clear from **Interaction 4.2.1**, that the size of the retinal image of an object of fixed size will vary with changes in its distance from an observer (sometimes called viewing distance). This means that we can get no firm indication of the size of an object from its retinal size alone; that size must be *scaled* for distance. Because individuals have no way of visually estimating size, except through scaling retinal size for distance, retinal size is a pivotal variable in perception. Measuring directly the retinal size of an object—the physical size of its images on the retinae—is both difficult and tedious. It is not difficult, then, to imagine the usefulness of an index, directly related to retinal size, that does not involve complex measurement procedures.

Visual angle is just such an index. It is broadly defined by the angle between two rays of light reaching the eye from any two points of interest in visual space. It is common to define the visual angle subtended by an object, or parts of an object, in which case the visual angle expresses the angular distance between its defined extremities, or limits of interest.

Thus, visual angle can be measured from the top to the bottom of an object (its vertical extent), from the left to the right of an object (its horizontal extent), or on any other axis of interest. In Interaction 4.2.1, for instance, you can explore the visual angle subtended by the *vertical* extent of the football player at various distances, but we could have easily quantified and expressed his *horizontal* extent. Note that, although we tend to focus on the visual angle subtended by *objects*, it is sometimes useful to express the retinal distance *between objects* (or point locations) in similar terms. Visual angle is a powerful and versatile measure. Its importance hinges on the fact that, in effect, it expresses the size of the retinal image. It has the virtue, then, that it takes into account the target's physical size and distance.

Visual angle is a very useful way of expressing the size of stimuli when describing, or reporting, perception experiments. When replicating experiments, it is sometimes easier, or desirable, to keep constant the visual angle subtended by a stimulus than to exactly reproduce stimulus size and/or viewing distance.

For convenience, the interactions in this unit express visual angle in terms of degrees (usually accurate to one or two decimal points), but you will find it expressed elsewhere in terms of degrees, minutes, and seconds of arc—the conventional units of angular measurement. So, keep in mind that there are 60 minutes in 1 degree, and 60 seconds in 1 minute of arc.

We have used the formula $\tan \alpha/2 = S/2D$ to calculate visual angle throughout this unit, but it is sometimes appropriate to use $\tan \alpha = S/D$ when the visual angle is relatively small (say, less than 10 degrees).

Students (and, sometimes, their teachers!) occasionally have difficulty visualizing appropriate size-distance relationships for a given visual angle. The sun and the moon subtend about half a degree of visual angle (despite the fact that the sun is vastly larger), whereas a quarter at arm's length subtends about 2 degrees of visual angle. The sun and the moon subtend roughly the same visual angle because the sun is, of course, much farther away (roughly 93 million miles versus 250,000 miles). In the preceding examples, the quarter subtends a visual angle four times that of the sun and the moon, because it is a mere arm's length from the observer. A quarter at 3 miles subtends a tiny 1 second of arc (1/360th of a degree).

As an object of fixed size moves away from an observer, it can assume any visual angle between about 180 degrees and virtually zero (that is, have a vast range of retinal sizes). Not only does that object not appear to shrink (as it would if size estimates were based solely on retinal size), but the observer can accurately report its actual size at any distance. This invariance of perceived height in the face of massive changes in visual angle is called *size constancy*. We are able to tell the correct size of objects independent of their retinal size. In fact, size constancy depends on our perception of depth and this makes our ability to automatically utilize depth cues to determine depth in the field of view a very valuable attribute indeed. We scale the retinal size of objects according to their apparent depth in the field of view. The golf ball in **Interaction 4.2.4** always looks smaller than the tennis ball, even when the former subtends a greater visual angle, because we know it to be closer.

If depth cues are reduced, or removed, or if they are contrived to be misleading, depth can be misperceived and size constancy breaks down. The results can be quite bizarre—as observation of an Ames room makes plain. As depth cues are systematically reduced, observers place increasingly greater reliance on retinal size (visual angle) as a cue to actual size. Shape constancy breaks down entirely; we are unable to discount the variations in retinal size due to changes in viewing distance.

The sun and the moon appear roughly the same size because we have virtually no cues to their depths in the field of view. We judge them as much the same size because they have roughly the same visual angle (the same retinal size). In the absence of adequate cues to depth, the law of visual angle applies: perceived size is wholly determined by visual angle.

Interaction 4.2.5 provides an unusual, aftereffect-predicated, demonstration of size-distance scaling. After prolonged inspection of an object against a contrasting surface, you can experience a strong negative afterimage. The perceived size of that afterimage varies with the distance to the surface against which it is viewed or "projected." The greater the distance, the larger the afterimage and vice versa.

This phenomenon was first demonstrated by Emmert in 1881, who expressed it mathematically: the perceived size of the afterimage (S_p) is a constant (k) times the product of the size of the retinal image (S_r) and the perceived distance of the afterimage (D_p): $S_p = k(S_r \times D_p)$. This relationship is modeled in **Interaction 4.2.6**.

In fact, this same equation can be used to formalize the principle of *size constancy*: as an object recedes into the distance, its retinal size (S_r) diminishes, but its perceived distance (D_p) increases. Their product ($S_r \times D_p$) remains constant, with the net result that perceived size (S_p) remains constant.

Unit 4.3 Size, Distance, and Other Illusions

4.3.1 The Müller-Lyer Illusion
4.3.2 The Poggendorff Illusion
4.3.3 The Ponzo Illusion
4.3.4 The Zöllner Illusion
4.3.5 The Dumbbell Müller-Lyer Illusion
4.3.6 The Horizontal-Vertical Illusion

This unit provides you with a set of data-gathering opportunities in which you can quantify the effects of several well-known illusions. You may find some of the illusions easier to "suppress" or "overcome" than others. In some cases, you will probably notice that the magnitude of an illusion will diminish in the course of several trials. Think about why that might be so.

Unit 4.2 focused on the intimate nexus between perceived size and distance. Observers are able to discount substantial changes in retinal size and achieve size constancy, provided they have adequate cues to depth. If veridical depth perception breaks down, as it can under impoverished viewing conditions, size perception can become bizarrely distorted—as in the case of the Ames room, where deliberate, but not apparent, distortion of the shape of a room and objects in it causes people in that room to appear grotesquely aberrant in size.

The Ames room leads an observer to believe that (say) two similarly sized people in it are at the same depth in the field of view when, in actuality, one is considerably closer than the other. Because, the closer one subtends a larger visual angle (at apparently the same depth), she or he looks bigger. In fact, many common visual illusions, including the moon illusion, result directly from a misperception of depth in the field of view and the consequent breakdown of veridical size-distance scaling.

Although appearing radically different, the Müller-Lyer illusion in **Interaction 4.3.1** is founded, arguably, on a similar principle to the moon illusion—misapplied size-distance scaling. In the classic Müller-Lyer illusion, the two central lines have the same visual angle, but appear different in size because they are different in apparent depth. In Interaction 4.3.1, the logic is reversed. The lines probably will be different in length when they appear equal in length, because you perceive them to be at different depths. This difference in length when the lines appear equal is, in effect, an index of the magnitude of the apparent difference in depth generated by the arrowheads.

Converging arrowheads arguably set up perspective cues that tend to make a line look closer than it is in actuality (remember, after all, that both the variable and standard stimuli are at the same depth—in the plane of the screen). Diverging arrowheads tend to make a central line appear farther away than it is, hence longer than it actually is.

In this sense, the Ames room, the moon illusion, and the Müller-Lyer illusion derive from the same source: misapplied size constancy scaling. Richard Gregory, a noted British perceptionist, advanced this explanation of the Müller-Lyer illusion as early as 1966. His general point was that size-distance scaling—so powerful and useful in maintaining stable perceptions in a three-dimensional world—can create illusions when misapplied to figures on two-dimensional surfaces. It is not necessary that these apparent differences in depth be consciously noted for an illusion to occur. As we saw in Unit 4.2, the processing of depth cues tends to be automatic, that is, seldom conscious or volitional.

It is not surprising that later investigators sought to use other line terminators (arguably devoid of perspective, or depth, cues) in order to check Gregory's explanation. The "dumbbell" versions of the illusion presented in Interactions 4.3.5 and 5.7.6 are cases in point. The real issue here is not whether the terminators contain *perspective* cues per se, but whether they contain misleading implicit depth cues. It is one of the frustrations and delights of experimental perception that, after more than 100 years (it was devised by Franz Müller-Lyer in 1889) the explanation of this simple, powerful illusion is still being hotly debated (for example, DeLucia & Hochberg, 1985, 1986, 1991; Pollack & Jaeger, 1991; Pressey & Pressey, 1992).

As Schiffman (1996, pp. 272–273) points out, the Poggendorff illusion in **Interaction 4.3.2** and the Zöllner illusion in **Interaction 4.3.4** have common historical, as well as theoretical, roots. J.C. Poggendorff was the editor of a journal to which Zöllner, an astronomer, submitted a monograph detailing an illusion he had noticed in a sample design printed on cloth. In Zöllner's illusion, parallel lines transected by short diagonals appear to diverge. Poggendorff observed another effect: apparent misalignment of the diagonals on each side of the parallel lines (Coren & Girgus, 1978).

Some wry commentators have noted that there are nearly as many theories about the Poggendorff illusion as there are psychologists who have devoted attention to it (for example, Levine & Shefner, 1991). Barbara Gillam (1971, 1980) has, nevertheless, convincingly argued that apparent depth is depicted in the Poggendorff configuration, and that the illusion is caused by the two oblique line segments appearing to lie on different depth planes. If this were so, those depth differences would be expected to disrupt the perceived alignment of the line segments. In this sense, the illusion would seem to be the result of a kind of misplaced perspective constancy.

A version of an illusion first devised in 1913 by Mario Ponzo is the basis for **Interaction 4.3.3**. Note that the strong pictorial perspective cues give a compelling, but false, impression of depth. The rod, or bar, closest to the point of convergence of the "parallel" lines usually appears longer than an equal-sized rod farther from that point. The illusion is an instance of misplaced, or inappropriate, size-distance scaling. When both rods subtend the same visual angle—that is, have the same physical and retinal size—the apparently more distant rod will appear bigger than the apparently closer one. Both rods have the same physical distance from the observer, so the automatic size-distance scaling is misplaced. The more compelling the depth cues, the stronger will be the illusion.

A convincing explanation of the extraordinarily powerful horizontal-vertical illusion has proven very elusive indeed. Like the other illusions in this unit, it has a very long history. It was first reported by Wilhelm Wundt in 1858. The horizontal-vertical illusion (which you can explore at your leisure in **Interaction 4.3.6**) is almost as old as experimental psychology itself. Why should the vertical bar always appear longer than the horizontal bar of equivalent length, sometimes by 30% or more? It is interesting to note that both the horizontal and the vertical bars contribute to the illusion: the horizontal appears shorter in the illusion context than in isolation; and the vertical appears longer in the context of the illusion than in isolation.

A point worth making here is that many of the illusions dealt with in this unit can be observed at work in real-world settings. They are by no means restricted to the rather abstract, reductionistic illustrations we and others have used to illustrate them. This is particularly so in the case of the horizontal-vertical illusion. There is a widespread overestimation of the vertical extent of everyday, real-world objects like trees, buildings, and parking meters (Chapanis & Mankin, 1967). Similar real-world Poggendorff-style and Müller-Lyer effects have been noted.

It is clear that there are wide individual differences in the extent to which observers see these illusions. Indeed, some observers do not see them at all. Age, gender, spatial skills, and education, for instance, are factors demonstrated to affect the perceived magnitude of the Poggendorff illusion, for example.

One methodological note: for convenience, illusion magnitude is expressed here as a number of screen *pixels*, rather than as conventional units of length, or displacement. We use this index in several interactions throughout *Exploring Perception*, so you need to be clear what is meant. The face of a computer monitor screen is divided into a matrix (or grid) of tiny, radiation-sensitive regions (or cells) called *pixels*. Each pixel can be separately addressed and/or activated using a computer program. Because, on a given screen, they have a (more or less) fixed size and spacing, counting the number of pixels can provide a reliable comparative index of distance, or area. The spacing of pixels varies from monitor to monitor, so comparison of data across unmatched monitors can be tricky. Pixel width varies from about 0.25 mm to 0.31 mm in modern monitors.

Unit 4.4 Stereoscopic Depth Perception

4.4.1 Binocular Disparity
4.4.2 The Horopter and Corresponding Points
4.4.3 Disparity and Retinal Location
4.4.4 Retinal Disparity and Object Depth
4.4.5 Disparity and Viewing Distance
4.4.6 Crossed and Uncrossed Disparity

In the first unit in this module, several interactions dealt with a range of depth cues, both monocular and binocular. One binocular depth cue not dealt with there, but nevertheless very important (particularly as a cue to the depth of objects relatively near in the field of view) is *binocular disparity*. This cue derives from the fact that the retinal images in each eye are slightly different. This is because our frontally directed eyes are laterally separated by about 65 mm and, accordingly, each has a slightly different view of the same scene.

This should be strikingly apparent if you hold one finger up about 7 or 8 inches in front of your nose and the other directly ahead at arm's length and view them carefully—first with your right eye, then with the left. Then try rapidly alternating the viewing eye. You will be struck by just how different the views of the two eyes are. The visual system has a remarkable ability to make use of this difference, or disparity, as a depth cue.

Many students find the principles of stereoscopic depth perception quite challenging. Part of the reason is the natural tendency to take depth perception for granted. The brain combines the images, or information, from the two eyes in such a way that it conceals the differences between them. We typically observe a single, seamless image and seldom stop to study how the images in our two eyes differ, or to analyze the information those differences carry, or encode, in various conditions. Virtually all of the interactions in this unit should suggest to you tiny, 1-minute, observational experiments you can make with no equipment beyond your hands and arms. Don't be afraid to experiment;

your family and friends will excuse you looking a little daft and preoccupied from time to time in the interests of science!

Interaction 4.4.1 provides you with a simple demonstration that binocular disparity—the difference in the left and right retinal images—diminishes rapidly as viewing distance increases, and its importance as a depth cue varies accordingly.

You can check out the fact that binocular disparity decreases with distance by closely observing objects in the world around you—one eye at a time. Note that with objects up close (1 to 2 feet away) the images in the two eyes are markedly different. This difference diminishes with distance. Try it. With objects 4 or 5 meters (about 13 to 16 feet) away you will find it difficult to discern any differences in the two eyes' views.

The important concepts of the *horopter* and *corresponding retinal points* are introduced in **Interaction 4.4.2**. Take the time to master them; they are central to virtually all other interactions in this unit. The horopter is an imaginary curved planar surface, which passes through the fixation point and is the locus of all points equidistant from the observer—that is, all points that have the same convergence angle and project to corresponding retinal points. Note that every fixation point, in effect, specifies an horopter. When the images of an object fall on corresponding points on the retinae, those images are fused by the visual system and are seen as a single object. There is a different set of corresponding points, a different horopter, for every fixation distance.

In general terms, the images of objects that do not fall on the horopter for a given fixation point—that is, objects closer or farther way than the fixation point—do not fall on corresponding points and are not fused. They generate double images, or *diplopia*. Retinal disparity exists. We are able to make use of this disparity to make assumptions about the relative depth of objects in the field of view.

In general terms, noncorresponding points are *diplopic*, yielding double images, but it is possible to fuse noncorresponding points that fall in a narrow region either side of the horopter. This region, in which images falling on (stimulating) noncorresponding points on the retinae are fused, is known as *Panum's fusional area*. Objects lying just off the horopter, in Panum's fusional area, are fused and yield single images, but they are discernibly different in depth from the fixation point and other points on the horopter.

As we have seen, objects lying outside Panum's fusional area are not fused, but diplopic. They are said to be in *crossed* or *uncrossed disparity* with respect to the fixation point. You have the opportunity to explore both notions in **Interaction 4.4.6**. Students sometimes find this notion of diplopia difficult to grasp, not least because we tend to be unaware that the vast bulk of nonfixated objects in the field of view are in fact diplopic. Perception of these double images is usually suppressed. This diplopia should become readily apparent, however, if you again hold one finger up about 7 or 8 inches in front of your nose and the other directly ahead at arm's length. This time fixate the front finger with both eyes open. You should see two images of the more distant finger. Then fixate the more distant finger. You should see two (diplopic) images of the closer finger. What you are observing, here, is the fact that the separate retinal images of an object not on the horopter (and outside Panum's fusional area) are not fused into a single image, but remain diplopic.

That simple observation also illustrates the notions of *crossed* and *uncrossed disparity*. When the closer finger is fixated and the more distant finger is diplopic, the latter is said to be in *uncrossed* disparity with the fixation point. When the more distant finger is fixated and the closer finger is diplopic, the latter is said to be in *crossed* disparity with respect to fixation.

Note that whether an object is seen in crossed or uncrossed disparity provides a relative depth cue: if an object is in *crossed* disparity it is *closer* to the observer than a fixated object or point. If it is in *uncrossed* disparity it is *more distant* than the fixation point. These relationships should be clearer to you as you work through Interaction 4.4.6. Remember, in both cases, the images of the nonfixated object are falling on noncorresponding points.

Interaction 4.4.3 enables you to explore the relationship between the relative depth of two objects in the field of view and the location of their images on the retinae. When objects are at the same depth, their images fall on corresponding points but, as soon as their depths differ, their images fall on noncorresponding points—retinal disparity is induced.

As **Interaction 4.4.4** demonstrates, if two objects are at different depths in the field of view, the amount by which their images are separated will be slightly different on your two retinae. As this difference in depth between the two objects increases, retinal disparity will increase. Retinal disparity is, thus, a powerful depth cue.

Again, you can observe this principle in action quite simply. Hold your left index finger 6 or 7 inches in front of your nose and your right index finger about 4 inches behind it and an inch or two to the right. Look at your fingers first with your right eye, then with your left. You will note that the separation of your fingers is much greater in the right eye's image. Retinal disparity exists because your fingers are at different depths. Now increase the difference in depth between your fingers by moving your right index finger back another 6 or 7 inches. The difference in separation will have increased dramatically. Finally, hold both fingers at the same depth, about 10 inches from your nose. View them with one eye, then the other. Note that their separation is identical in the two images. There is no retinal disparity because there is no difference in depth.

Interaction 4.4.5 provides you with the opportunity to see how retinal disparity varies with viewing distance when objects are separated in depth by a fixed distance.

Unit 4.5 Space Perception

4.5.1 Motion Parallax
4.5.2 Kinetic Depth Effect
4.5.3 Motion Perspective and Optical Flow
4.5.4 Stereo-Motion as a Depth Cue
4.5.5 Motion Parallax and Object Form
4.5.6 Disparity and Motion Parallax

A vital source of information about the disposition (or relative locations) of objects in three-dimensional space is their motion relative to each other when they move, the observer moves, or when both move at different rates and/or in different directions. These monocular, movement-produced, depth cues are known collectively as *motion parallax*. Motion allows an observer to compare and integrate several different images of a scene over time. The patterns of motion that emerge can be highly informative. When an observer is in motion relative to stationary objects, one of which is fixated, those objects closer than the fixation point will appear to move in the direction opposite the observer's movement. Objects farther away than fixation appear to move in the same direction as the observer. Motion parallax thus provides valuable information about the relative depth of objects in the field of view. You have the opportunity to explore both observer-generated and object-generated motion parallax in **Interaction 4.5.1**.

In addition to information regarding the relative *direction* of motion of objects in the field of view, humans are also able to utilize data on relative speed of motion to make inferences regarding the depth of objects in the field of view. In general terms, the closer an object, the faster will be its rate of translation across the retina of the observer.

It is not uncommon for people to move their heads back and forth to judge better the relative distance of near objects in particular. They are, in effect, generating motion parallax and the information that comes with it.

You can experience quite powerful motion parallax by simply pivoting, or rotating, your head without moving your neck or torso. Hold up the index finger of your left hand about 7 or 8 inches in front of your nose, and the index finger of your right hand straight ahead at arm's length; and rotate your head from side to side with one eye closed (remember motion parallax is a monocular depth cue). If you fixate on the far finger, the near one will move in the direction opposite your head movement. If you fixate on the near finger, the image of the far finger will appear to move in the direction of your head movement. If you fixate on an object beyond both fingers they will both appear to move in the direction opposite your head movement. Observe closely and you will notice that the near finger appears to be moving much more rapidly than the far finger in this condition.

Interaction 4.5.2 illustrates a special class of motion parallax called the *kinetic depth effect*. Not only can humans (and a number of other species) make use of the relative motion between objects, but they can utilize information regarding the relative motion of parts of an object to make inferences about its shape. As an object moves or rotates, it is possible to integrate the various views afforded into a coherent, unified percept of its three-dimensional structure. In Interaction 4.5.2, four objects have identical two-dimensional profiles, or shapes, when viewed in side elevation. When those objects are rotated, information is generated about their three dimensional structure, or shape.

A second class of monocular, motion-produced, depth cue is *motion perspective* or *optic flow* (see **Interaction 4.5.3**). Very effective use is made of this class of depth cue in computer games, particularly those that simulate cars, or motorcycles, racing on speedways. Motion perspective is a powerful source of information on both depth in the field of view and velocity of movement. As an observer moves forward through the world, predictable changes occur in the optical array. Contours and details appear to slowly flow, or fan, outward from the fixation point, then flow past the observer at an accelerating rate. The reverse is true, of course, if an observer moves backward through the environment: contours converge on and ultimately merge with the fixation point. You may find it instructive to analyze carefully how the impressively strong illusions of both depth and movement are generated in video game arrays. You might even enjoy spending time trying to observe the principles of motion perspective at work!

Throughout this module, we deal with depth cues more or less discretely, in isolation. In practice, however, many different depth cues can be present in a scene and codetermine an observer's estimate of depth. This begs the question as to how (on what basis) depth cues are combined. In general terms, the effects of depth cues appear to be additive. Occasionally, however, cues appear to combine to yield emergent, higher-order depth cues. Stereo-motion of the kind dealt with in **Interaction 4.5.4** is one such case in point. It appears to derive from differences and similarities in the relative rates of motion across the retinae of the images of a moving object. Stereo-motion appears to have clear implications for the signaling of danger. For instance, Interaction 4.5.4 makes it clear that if the rate of change of location of the image of a moving object is the same on both retinae, that object is moving directly toward the observer. If that rate of change of location is both substantial and equal in both retinae, the moving object is potentially on a dangerous collision course. Conversely, if the rate of change of location is different in the two eyes, this is consistent with an object moving obliquely and likely to miss the observer. Stereo-motion involves comparison of the rates of change of location in the two eyes and is, in this sense, a higher order depth cue. It is, of course, necessarily a binocular depth cue.

As noted, Interactions 4.5.1 and 4.5.2 deal with motion parallax and a phenomenon that appears to be a special case of motion parallax: the kinetic depth effect. **Interaction 4.5.5** enables you to explore a third, related phenomenon. Not only is information regarding three-dimensional shape usually generated when an object moves (particularly when it rotates), but analogous information is gained as an observer moves relative to a target object. As we saw in the case of the kinetic depth effect, humans are capable of integrating several two-dimensional views distributed in time into a single, stable percept of a three-dimensional object. The same is true when the viewpoint of a moving observer changes.

Unit 4.4 explores binocular disparity in some detail. Significantly, another term for binocular disparity is *binocular parallax*. This terminology hints at the close nexus between motion parallax and binocular disparity, which is exemplified in the final interaction in this unit. The purpose of **Interaction 4.5.6** is to demonstrate the formal equivalence of the monocular information generated by motion parallax and that available with conventional binocular viewing. By integrating information over time, an observer with only one functioning eye can generate nontrivial depth information of essentially the same class as that available via binocular disparity.

Unit 4.6 Lightness, Brightness, and Contrast

4.6.1 Dark Adaptation of Rods and Cones
4.6.2 Stimulus Intensity and Brightness
4.6.3 Mach Bands
4.6.4 The Purkinje Shift
4.6.5 Bloch's Law and Ricco's Law
4.6.6 Piper's Law

In one sense, humans have two visual systems—a principle first proposed by J. von Kries in 1896. The two photoreceptor types found in the human retina—rods and cones—not only have distinctive shapes and spatial distributions, they also have markedly different functions and properties. Rods are specialized for operation in reduced light, under so-called *scotopic* viewing conditions. Night vision is essentially rod vision. It is also achromatic. The cones, critical to color vision, are nonfunctional in scotopic conditions. They are specialized for daylight (or *photopic*) viewing. Humans, thus, have a visual system able to function well by day and by night. It takes some time, however, to effect the transition between these two visual systems—to *dark adapt* and to *light adapt*. Interaction 4.6.1 provides you with the opportunity to explore the former in some detail.

When you walk into a darkened room, a cinema for instance, it takes some time for your eyes to become accustomed to the dark. You experience a kind of transitory blindness. But exposure to the dark has the remarkable property of increasing the retina's sensitivity to light. The longer you spend in the dark, the more sensitive to light your eyes become. Your threshold for the detection of visual stimulation diminishes. Eventually, provided there is some ambient illumination, you will come to see quite well in a room that initially appeared pitch black, without discernible contour or detail. This is the process of dark adaptation with which we are all familiar.

It is usual to begin dark adaptation experiments with a fully light-adapted eye. Light-adapted cones are much more sensitive to light than light-adapted rods. Not only are cones more sensitive to begin with, they adapt more rapidly than cones during the first 3 or 4 minutes after illumination is extinguished. Cone threshold diminishes briskly during this phase—that is, sensitivity increases markedly. Threshold and sensitivity are, of course, two sides of the same coin; as sensitivity increases, threshold decreases, and vice versa.

The rods are adapting also, but from a higher light-adapted threshold and at a slower rate. Thus, rod and cone adaptation are occurring in parallel. Both are initiated at the onset of darkness and have different time courses, or what might be called different *threshold reduction profiles*. We detect using the more sensitive of the two visual systems at any point in time. Cones are initially more sensitive, but that sensitivity plateaus rapidly after the initial steep increase. Rods start from a higher threshold and sensitivity increases more slowly than with cones, but rods go on adapting for much longer. Thus, after about 7 to 10 minutes in the dark, rods are absolutely more sensitive than cones and they mediate detection. The increase in sensitivity resulting from cone adaptation has plateaued after 3 or 4 minutes, whereas the rods continue to adapt for 25 to 30 minutes.

In **Interaction 4.6.1**, rod and cone adaptation are simulated independently and then in parallel. What should become clear is that dark adaptation has two distinct phases: a first phase, where detection is mediated by the cones, which both start out more sensitive and adapt quicker; and a second phase, where detection is mediated by the rods, which dark-adapt more slowly from a higher threshold, but go on adapting longer. Dark adaptation is a remarkable process: dark-adapted sensitivity is some 100,000 times greater than light-adapted sensitivity.

So far we have noted several differences between the rods and cones in terms of their shape, spatial distribution on the retina, dark-adaptation profiles, and so on. They differ also in their sensitivity to light of different wavelengths. The two kinds of photoreceptors are not equally responsive to (sensitive to) light across the visible spectrum. In general terms, the rods require less radiant light energy than cones to reach threshold at all wavelengths except very long ones—beyond about 650 nm.

The lowest threshold for scotopic vision occurs around 500 nm. The rods are most sensitive to electromagnetic radiation of that wavelength. The lowest threshold for cone-mediated photopic vision is in the yellow-green range at around 550 nm. During dark adaptation, humans shift from photopic (cone) to scotopic (rod) vision. This will be accompanied by corresponding changes in the relative brightness of lights of different wavelength. In particular, one would expect light in the blue range (around 500 nm) to appear brighter after dark adaptation (the rods are maximally sensitive to 500-nm light) than longer wavelength light (corresponding to red).

Some interesting perceptual consequences of the different spectral sensitivities of rods and cones are readily observable. One, the *Purkinje shift*, is simulated in **Interaction 4.6.4**. Johannes Purkinje, a Czech physiologist, first described the phenomenon in 1825. In Interaction 4.6.4, the equally bright red and blue spots appear differentially bright post–dark adaptation because of the particular sensitivity of rods to short wavelength stimulation and their relative insensitivity to light at the red (long wavelength) end of the spectrum. There is, then, a change in the brightness of light of certain wavelengths as a direct consequence of the shift from photopic to scotopic vision, and vice versa. As Schiffman (1996, p. 93) picturesquely puts it: as twilight progresses, blues and greens will change to moonlight grays and reds to moonlight blacks.

As you will see in **Interaction 4.6.3**, considerations of adaptation and wavelength aside, brightness seldom matches the actual distribution of light intensity across a surface. In that interaction, intensity is constant across the surface of each of the five achromatic panels, but there appears to be a bright band on the brighter side of each join and a dark band on the darker side. These are known as *Mach bands.* They are almost certainly attributable to lateral antagonism of the kind detailed in Interactions 1.5.1 to 1.5.3.

It is not unusual in psychophysics to vary a stimulus parameter until a comparison stimulus is just noticeably different from a standard. You will have the opportunity to explore these *just noticeable differences*—sometimes called *difference thresholds* or *difference limens*—in several interactions in Module 5. When investigating the detectability of a stimulus, or differences between stimuli, it is usual to make minimal changes in one variable at a time. Sometimes, however, several stimulus parameters are changed simultaneously, while keeping the total stimulus energy constant.

Consider the detection of a small circular patch of light. The total energy coming from the patch, or spot, depends on stimulus intensity (*radiance*), stimulus area, and stimulus duration. Total energy is, in effect, the product of these three stimulus values. Trade-off relationships exist between these variables, such that the stimulus energy can be kept constant, using a wide range of possible parameter combinations. The total stimulus energy value of most theoretical interest relates to threshold energy. These trade-off relationships can be explored, in detail, for various pairwise combinations of the stimulus parameters (intensity, duration, and area) in **Interactions 4.6.5** and **4.6.6**. Those relationships are expressed in three laws: *Bloch's law, Ricco's law,* and *Piper's law.* In all three cases, we focus on the critical energy level (C) corresponding to absolute threshold, but, in general terms, stimuli with the same product of intensity, duration, and area will be equally detectable.

If stimulus duration is held constant (all flashes of light last a fixed amount of time), then the total stimulus energy (C) will be the product of the stimulus area (A) and stimulus intensity (I). This relationship $C = I \times A$ is known as *Ricco's law.* Thus, for instance, it requires half the radiance to detect a spot of light twice as large. The total energy required for detection is the same, whether the spot is small and bright or large and dull. What is critical, within limits, is the total light energy. Observers are able to discriminate between the two stimuli, of course, but their detectability is the same. Ricco's law holds only for small spots of light; beyond a certain size, additional area conveys no advantage.

Bloch's law, in contrast, assumes stimulus area is held constant and expresses the relationship between duration and intensity. The critical amount of energy required for detection is the product of duration and intensity. Thus, Bloch's law can be expressed as $C = I \times T$. Put differently, the threshold intensity (radiance) required for detection is inversely related to stimulus duration. The more intense the stimulus, the shorter the required flash of light. In the same way, the longer the flash of light, the less is the required intensity. Again, the total energy required for detection is a constant, regardless of how it is distributed in time and, again, the generalization is bounded. There is an upper limit of about 0.10 second on stimulus duration. Exposure for longer durations confers no additional advantage and threshold is determined by stimulus intensity only. Be aware that Bloch's law is occasionally referred to as the Bunsen-Roscoe law.

As noted, Ricco's law holds for only small stimuli. Stimulus areas greater than 10 minutes of arc are subject to *Piper's law.* In this case, the constant visual effect required for detection (C) is the product of stimulus intensity (I), and the *square root of the stimulus area,* ($\sqrt{A}$). Piper's law is dealt with in Interaction 4.6.6.

In both Interactions 4.6.5 and 4.6.6, the constant visual effect or energy (C) required for detection is represented by the area of the defined rectangle in each case. That area remains invariant despite changes in stimulus parameters I, T, and A.

Intensity, duration, and area may be thought of, then, as factors affecting absolute threshold for the detection of visual stimuli. Note that Ricco's law holds only for stimulation of relatively small areas of the central retina, whereas Bloch's law best describes detection in the periphery of the retina. Bloch's law may have a familiar ring to it for those students interested in photography. The trade-off between time and intensity is pivotal when taking photographs. Similar results can be achieved by trading time for intensity on dull days and bright. A brief film exposure on a bright day will achieve much the same result as a long exposure on dull days. Proper exposure requires the same total amount of energy whatever the lighting conditions.

Unit 4.7 Gratings and Spatial Frequency Analysis

You may find the interactions in this unit rather abstract. They may seem to you to have little relevance, or relationship, to the study of visual perception as you know it. Many of the terms will be unfamiliar to you. But, although some of this material may seem a little arcane at first, the approach to visual perception that it will eventually make accessible is important and (ultimately) quite fascinating.

This unit provides you with some of the main concepts and tools of *spatial frequency analysis*, which provides a powerful way of specifying a visual scene. It provides an unusual way of specifying the commonplace. It does so in a way that has yielded some interesting insights into human visual information processing. There is good evidence that spatial frequency analysis may well be the way that the visual system processes information about the visual scene. You will find out (I hope) that spatial frequency analysis provides not only elegant *description*, but may also contain the germ of some good *explanations*.

Spatial frequency has a precise technical meaning that we will come to in a moment, but when applied to the analysis of a visual scene it generally refers to how *fine-grained* or *coarse-grained* that scene is. Think of a scene in monochrome, with spatially distributed patterns of black, white, and intermediate grays. Is the scene made up of large, dominant, coarse-grained objects or fine, detailed, fine-grained ones? Most likely it is a mixture of both. In general terms, the large objects are said to be the low spatial frequency ("few-and-big") components of the picture and the fine-grained objects ("many-and-small") are termed the high spatial frequency components.

The key principle on which spatial frequency analysis is founded was first explicated by French mathematician J. B. Fourier. He argued that you can analyze any complex spatial pattern of light intensities into a series of simpler sine-wave (sinusoidal) patterns. These underlying patterns are regular, smoothly modulated patterns of light and dark—that is, they are gratings. Thus, by adding together various gratings, we can produce any pattern of light distribution. Conversely, we can take any pattern, or any complex spatial distribution of light, and transform it into its simple component sine-waves. These elemental constituents are called the Fourier components of the target pattern or scene. This transformation is accomplished mathematically using a technique based on Fourier's theorem.

If we had a range of detector cells, which were tuned to respond to various spatial frequencies in an input scene, their activity, in combination, could form the basis of visual pattern perception. Each scene, or stimulus, would be analyzed, thus, into its spatial frequency components by detectors in the nervous system tuned to fire to specified spatial frequencies. Their combined activity might form the neural substrate of perception.

Much of the research on the ability of the visual system to detect spatial frequencies has used achromatic grating stimuli of the kind used throughout Unit 4.7. It is necessary, then, to be able to specify precisely the properties of such gratings. In particular, we need to be able to specify the *waveform*, *contrast*, *spatial frequency*, *phase*, and *orientation* of such gratings. Gratings are useful to the extent that they can be thought of as the basic building blocks for any complex pattern or scene. **Interaction 4.7.1** enables you explore each grating attribute or property. When you have worked through that interaction, you should be able to describe the main features of most grating stimuli with ease. In this sense, Interaction 4.7.1 provides you with a good part of the basic vocabulary of spatial frequency analysis.

There are many different waveforms possible (including triangle-wave and sawtooth gratings), but Interaction 4.7.1 deals only with square-wave and sine-wave gratings. In general, gratings are named in terms of the shape of the intensity distribution, or profile, across their surface.

You will continue to encounter the distinction between sine-wave and square-wave gratings throughout this unit, so spend some time in the beginning getting the difference straight. As noted, gratings vary in the distribution of intensity across their surface. In the case of square waves, intensity changes abruptly at the boundaries of the light and dark bars, generating sharp contours, or edges. In the case of sine-wave gratings, intensity changes more gradually (sinusoidally), giving rise to fuzzy borders between the light and dark bars of the grating. The intensity distribution follows a sine-wave function.

Earlier, we referred to stimuli as fine- and coarse-grained. We are able to characterize gratings more precisely. A *cycle* consists of one light bar and one dark bar. Varying the number of cycles in a grating of fixed size will affect the spatial frequency. Spatial frequency is usually expressed in terms of the number of *cycles* the grating contains per unit distance on the retina. As seen in earlier units of the module, visual angle is a very convenient way of specifying retinal size (see Interactions 4.2.2 to 4.2.4). So, spatial frequency is usually expressed in *cycles per degree* of visual angle.

Interaction 4.7.2 allows you to vary, first, the number of cycles in a grating and, second, spatial frequency. A fine-grained grating is said to have a high-spatial frequency; a coarse-grained grating is generally held to have a low-spatial frequency.

It is important that you develop an intuitive feel for the way in which spatial frequency varies with distance. The spatial frequency of a fixed grating will decrease as you move toward it. This is because visual angle increases as viewing distance decreases. Because spatial frequency is calculated by dividing the number of grating cycles by the visual angle, the larger the visual angle the lower will be the spatial frequency (in cycles/degree of visual angle). The virtue of relating the unit of spatial frequency to the size of the retinal image, using visual angle, is that it avoids the need to specify the size of contrasting areas and the viewing distance.

In the same way, the spatial frequency of a fixed grating will increase as viewing distance increases. Visual angle reduces with viewing distance. Again, because spatial frequency is calculated by dividing the number of grating cycles by the visual angle, the smaller the visual angle the higher will be the spatial frequency. Another way of increasing the spatial frequency of a grating of *fixed* size is, of course, to increase the number of cycles it contains (that is, the number of pairs of dark and light bars). **Interaction 4.7.4** allows you to explore how spatial frequency varies with viewing distance. Take the time to understand the calculations; they are not difficult and will help consolidate some useful concepts.

Take special note that we enable you to *magnify* the 1-degree image in Interaction 4.7.2 so that you might better see the consequences of increasing the number of cycles, but it still remains a "1-degree" image for the purpose of calculating spatial frequency in this interaction. You might find this a little confusing because in the "real world," of course, magnifying a grating reduces its spatial frequency. Just keep in mind, here, that we are discussing a 1-degree grating, which is shown larger than its actual size to make observation easier.

An important property of gratings is the relative intensity of the light and dark bars. Interaction 4.7.1 should help you get a general "feel" for what is meant by contrast. Details of how it is specified and calculated are given in **Interaction 4.7.5**. Contrast is high when the difference in intensity between the light and dark bars is great. At very low levels of contrast, individual bars may not be visible. There are several ways of calculating the contrast of a grating, but Interaction 4.7.5 focuses on the commonly used *Michaelson's contrast ratio.* This is the maximum intensity value (I_{max}), minus the minimum intensity value (I_{min}), divided by the sum of the two:

$$(I_{max} - I_{min}) / (I_{max} + I_{min})$$

When working through Interaction 4.7.5, be sure to always select a maximum intensity value for the grating that is greater than the minimum.

The power of Fourier's idea can be illustrated by the fact that summing regular, smooth, sinusoidal gratings can yield sharp, clean edges—such as those we see in square-wave gratings. **Interaction 4.7.6** enables you to sum many simple sine-wave gratings to build a square-wave grating. If you sum all of the odd multiples of the fundamental sine-wave frequency the result will be a square wave.

Hopefully, Interaction 4.7.6 will give you some feel for the power of Fourier's insight and the potential spatial frequency analysis has for describing the properties of even the most complex scenes and patterns. At base, it consists in the view that any complex visual scene is a mosaic of dark and light that can be expressed in terms of the frequency of a set of component sinusoids and their corresponding contrasts.

Unit 4.8 Contextual Effects and Apparent Brightness

4.8.1 Intensity and Brightness
4.8.2 Adaptation to Spatial Frequency
4.8.3 Adaptation and Contrast Sensitivity
4.8.4 Simultaneous Brightness Contrast
4.8.5 Brightness-Darkness Independence
4.8.6 Frequency Spectra of Sinusoids

Brightness—the psychological correlate of the intensity of a visual stimulus—seldom reflects the actual distribution of physical light intensity across a surface. The surroundings of a test patch can affect its perceived brightness. This is exemplified in this unit in the cases of Mach bands (Interaction 4.8.1) and simultaneous brightness contrast (Interaction 4.8.4). In **Interaction 4.8.1**, you can plot the notional light intensity and brightness profiles of a test patch that gives rise to Mach bands. Pay special attention to the differences between those two plots. The physical intensity profile clearly does not contain any counterpart for Mach bands, consistent with the fact that brightness seldom matches physical intensity across a surface.

Interaction 4.6.3, in Unit 4.6, also investigates Mach bands, providing an explanation of the processes that might give rise to them. You might find it useful to spend some time integrating the commentaries each provides on the operation of the visual system.

In *simultaneous brightness contrast,* the brightness of a test patch again is affected by the intensity of its background. **Interaction 4.8.4** provides the opportunity to compare the intensity and brightness profiles of the test patch and surround. Again, study carefully where the two profiles coincide and where they diverge. This interaction also makes it possible to equate the background intensities in the figure, while monitoring the way the brightness and intensity profiles change. This is a little complex, but it's worth the effort to try to understand the phenomenon at this level.

We dealt with the mechanics of dark adaptation in some detail in Interaction 4.6.1. The benefits of having a duplex visual system can be further explored in Interaction 4.8.3. Our visual system has both a wide *range of operation* and excellent *contrast sensitivity.* We can see well in both bright light (cone-mediated *photopic* vision) and very dim light (rod-mediated *scotopic* vision). This wide operational range is due not least to the ability to adapt to the dark. Remarkably, once we have dark-adapted, we can detect differences in light intensity of less than 1%—indexing excellent *contrast sensitivity* at low levels of intensity. **Interaction 4.8.3** is intended to give you a good sense of how our visual system achieves both good contrast sensitivity and a wide operating range.

Considerable use is made of the notion of *operating curves.* These relate light intensity to brightness. As pointed out in the interaction, the operating range is represented by the sloping portion of the operating curve. If that slope is shallow—if a small change in intensity causes only a small change in brightness—contrast sensitivity is poor. If a small change in intensity causes a large change in brightness, the system is said to have good contrast sensitivity.

The key point in Interaction 4.8.3 is that the human visual system achieves both a wide operating range and good contrast sensitivity by shifting the operating range to match the illumination level, through the processes of light and dark adaptation.

Interaction 4.8.5 consists of a simple demonstration, but one which provides a significant theoretical commentary. It shows that darkness and brightness processing are not two aspects of a single process, but that they are processed by two independent systems. This demonstration rests on the fact that we appear to be able to fatigue the darkness perception system and the brightness system *independently* and with discernible perceptual consequences. Prolonged exposure to a predominantly black-inducing figure fatigues the darkness system more than it does the brightness system. In contrast, exposure to a predominantly white figure fatigues the brightness system. When the darkness system is fatigued, for instance, the darkness response is diminished, causing dark black lines to be less visible and to appear finer.

The final interaction in this module, **Interaction 4.8.6**, returns briefly to the properties of gratings addressed in some detail in Unit 4.7. As outlined in that unit, Fourier formalized the view that any light pattern, or scene, can be expressed as the sum of a set of component sinusoidal gratings. Significantly, these components can be represented graphically as a spatial frequency spectrum that shows the level of contrast in a given pattern at various spatial frequencies—providing a very economical and powerful summary description of visual stimuli.

This interaction lets you select a spatial frequency and a contrast level and returns both the corresponding grating and a plot of grating luminance as a function of position. *Luminance* is the light coming from the surface. Pay special attention to the relative location of each stimulus pattern (grating) in the spatial frequency spectrum. Although the properties of a series of separate gratings is plotted in the same space for comparison purposes in this interaction, it is more usual to estimate a spatial frequency spectrum for a single, complex pattern or scene. The Fourier transform represents this kind of spatial pattern in terms of a set of component sinusoids. In essence, a spatial frequency spectrum of the kind plotted here summarizes how much contrast there is in a pattern, or scene, at each of the different component spatial frequencies. Thus, strictly, each scene has a distinctive spatial frequency spectrum. Each of the gratings plotted in this interaction, by comparison, has only a single spatial frequency and a single contrast. Each is represented by a single spike—the simplest possible spectrum. But it is possible to represent elegantly any pattern, however complex, in terms of its frequency spectrum—its component sinusoids and their corresponding contrasts. The example given in Interaction 4.7.6 shows, in effect, the component sinusoids of a square-wave grating pattern.

Module 5

Psychophysics

Unit 5.1 Measuring Sensory Experience

This unit provides a brief introduction to the central problem of *psychophysics*—quantification of the way in which psychological experience varies as a function of changes in physical stimulus properties. It emphasizes the inherent variability of stimulus, experience, and response (Interactions 5.1.1 and 5.1.2) and the sensitivity of observers, both to threshold stimulation and to the differences between stimuli (Interactions 5.1.3 to 5.1.5). Finally, the concept of a psychophysical function, which we frequently revisit in this module, is introduced in Interaction 5.1.6.

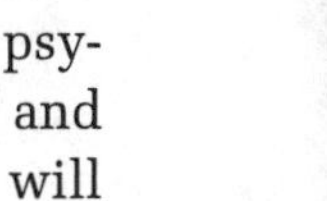

Interaction 5.1.1 is a simple interaction but, if you have a clear understanding of what it implies, you will be sensitive to several of the reasons why psychophysical experiments are necessarily constructed the way they are. There are three core messages in this first interaction: (i) that we cannot observe psychological experience directly—it must be inferred from observer responses; (ii) that the physical stimulus, psychological experience, and observer's response are all inherently and incurably variable; (iii) that the variability in observers' responses will inevitably be greater than the variability of the physical stimulus and the subjective experience because it necessarily includes both; and (iv) that experienced stimulus magnitude, or intensity, (typically) increases

more slowly than actual physical increases—that is, there is no simple 1:1 mapping of subjective experience to stimulus properties.

Given the inherent variability in stimulus, experience, and response, it is not surprising that psychophysical experiments usually consist of a daunting number of trials, as any number of bleary-eyed participants will attest. Over many trials, random errors should tend to sum to zero, yielding an accurate estimate of the mean response in each condition.

Interaction 5.1.2 should dispel any doubts you have about the fact that responses are variable and error-prone. Do as many trials as you can bear! If you do, you should get a reasonable check on whether your errors appear to be random or systematic. If they are random, you would expect them to be more or less normally distributed about the actual stimulus value. It is possible, of course, that you might systematically overestimate or underestimate. If you do, that should be clear when you plot your data.

The fact that errors are systematic does not necessarily reflect on the observer. Systematic errors can result from poorly designed, or poorly executed, experiments. Factors such as the relative locations of stimuli, their color, their relative frequency, and their order of presentation, for instance, can all systematically bias judgments; the list is a very long one.

As you work through the numerous data-gathering exercises in this module, and others, be critical of the way the tasks are constructed and presented. Some have stimulus conditions and presentation sequences rigorously counterbalanced and/or randomized; others are less rigorous (usually when the point being made in the interaction is not about method per se and/or where constant errors are not too important to the essential message being communicated). Most often, anomalies in your data will alert you to possible sources of bias and error. Go searching, be critical, and compare notes! Even the most careful and experienced psychophysicist can encounter unexpected sources of error.

You will encounter the notion of *absolute threshold*, first introduced in **Interaction 5.1.3**, throughout this module. The first thing that will become apparent to you is that absolute threshold—the minimum detectable level of stimulus energy—is not absolute! This should not be too surprising, given the emphasis on the inherent variability and error in psychophysical judgments. The series of interactions in Unit 5.3 outline an alternative approach to describing detection performance: *signal detection theory*. The unique power of that approach lies in the fact that it models detection as a probabilistic event related to the observer's sensitivity and the criterion adopted. As such, it is a significant advance of naive threshold models of detection. It recognizes the importance of variability in the system and the importance of human factors in decision making about the presence or absence of a stimulus.

Interaction 5.1.4 is a little complicated, but if you work through it systematically you will have the basis for a good understanding of the classical approach to deriving and interpreting *difference thresholds*. The approach outlined is of historical importance (mainly) and some of the concepts tend not to be used much in modern psychophysics. It provides, however, nice context, contrast, and counterpoint to current approaches.

It is often useful to know the smallest difference between two stimuli that just can be detected. For instance, how much longer than a standard line does a second line need to be for someone to judge it "longer"? This *just noticeable difference* is known as the difference threshold. You will have the opportunity to explore just noticeable differences informally in Interaction 5.1.5, but first look at what it means graphically in Interaction 5.1.4.

Interaction 5.1.4 assumes you want to establish the difference threshold of an ideal observer making judgments of line length. It is usual for the observer to contrast a variable stimulus (V_s) with a fixed standard line (S_s), judging which of the two is longer/shorter. In interaction 5.1.4, the Vs is a red line and the Ss a blue line. The aim of the experiment is to establish the minimum difference in their lengths that just can be detected by the observer. As you progressively increase the length of the variable red line (V_s) using the cursor, some idealized data will be generated for a series of comparisons between the V_s and S_s. Note that if you release the cursor at any time the graph will be completed for you automatically.

This plot can then be used to establish a difference threshold (ΔI) for the observer. Be sure to check how this is done, but first examine how the graph defines the point of subjective equality (PSE). As you will learn from the interaction, the PSE is defined by the point where the two functions cross. It is the length of the variable stimulus equally likely to be judged longer or shorter than the standard stimulus: the variable stimulus is judged to be smaller on one-half of the trials and larger on one-half. So, at the PSE, the two lines—variable and standard—appear to be equal in length. In the example given, subjective equality is reached when the variable stimulus is slightly smaller than the standard stimulus.

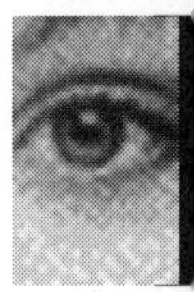

The difference threshold is defined as the minimum reliably detectable difference between two stimuli. In this case, it is shown by ΔI—the difference in length between the standard stimulus (S_s) and the variable stimulus (V_s) judged longer than it on 75% of trials. It is important that you understand why the 75% level is chosen: it represents the value of the variable stimulus at which a difference is noted one-half of the time. Don't worry too much about the *interval of uncertainty*; it is seldom used these days, but is included here for formal completeness (it has a venerable past but not much of a future!).

The interval of uncertainty is defined as the difference in magnitude between the stimulus judged greater than the standard 25% of the time and that judged greater 75% of the time. Understanding the logic and spirit of this approach is more important, in a sense, than understanding the detail.

The intention of **Interaction 5.1.5** is to help you develop a feel for the idea of a difference threshold or just noticeable difference. The way just noticeable differences are obtained in this interaction is not the way they are usually established experimentally; those methods are spelled out in Unit 5.2.

Interaction 5.1.6 introduces the *psychophysical function* and provides a simple example. You will encounter several psychophysical functions as you work through this module, so it is important you understand their virtues and how they are derived. The difference threshold for (say) lifted weights usually varies as a function of the magnitude of the weights used. To that extent, there is no single difference threshold value, but a family of them. Plots of these families of threshold values (say, the difference threshold as a function of the magnitude of the standard weight) are psychophysical functions. They powerfully summarize the operation of a sensory system, providing a spectrum of thresholds, across a range of conditions, rather than a single threshold. Not all psychophysical functions are plots of thresholds, of course.

Unit 5.2 Classical Psychophysical Methods

5.2.1 The Method of Limits
5.2.2 The Method of Limits and DL
5.2.3 Staircase Methods
5.2.4 The Method of Adjustment and PSE
5.2.5 The Method of Constant Stimuli
5.2.6 RT and Stimulus Discriminability

This unit focuses on the classical psychophysical methods for establishing absolute thresholds (Interactions 5.2.1 and 5.2.3); difference thresholds (Interaction 5.2.2 and 5.2.5); and points of subjective equality (Interaction 5.2.4). In the final interaction (5.2.6), reaction time is used as an index of the difficulty of making a simple stimulus discrimination.

In essence, all these psychophysical methods are focused on a single problem: establishing the quantitative relationship between physical environmental stimulation and the subjective sensory (psychological) experience. This task may sound easier than it is in fact.

As the first interaction in this module (Interaction 5.1.1) made clear, the psychological impact of variations in physical stimulation is not directly observable, or easily quantifiable, in a volatile system vulnerable to perturbation by a wide range of influences. The phenomenon of interest (sensory and perceptual experience) is not directly accessible to observation; it can only be inferred. Psychophysics, and most of its practical and philosophical dilemmas, has a history as long as experimental psychology itself.

The psychophysical methods explored in the unit—the method of limits (**Interactions 5.2.1** and **5.2.2**), the method of adjustment (**Interaction 5.2.4**), and the method of constant stimuli (**Interaction 5.2.5**)—were initially developed by Gustav T. Fechner in the late 1850s, culminating in a book published in German in 1860, *Elements of Psychophysics*. Fechner, a philosopher, physicist, and mathematician, is usually regarded as the father of psychophysics. Indeed, it was he who coined the term. The staircase method (**Interaction 5.2.3**) was developed some time later (Cornsweet, 1962), obviating some of the inefficiencies in Fechner's seminal procedure. There are many variants of the staircase method, itself a variant of the method of limits, some of bewildering complexity. Modern psychophysics has developed a wide range of modifications of Fechner's three original psychophysical methods (for a summary see, for example, Sekuler & Blake, 1994, pp. 493–497).

As you explore the texts, you may come across some conflicting terminology regarding these methods. The method of limits is sometimes referred to as the *method of minimal change*. The method of adjustment is occasionally called the *method of average error*.

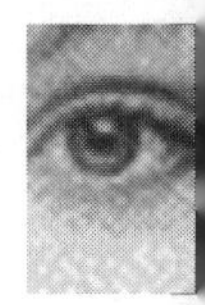

It is difficult to overestimate the importance of the formalization of psychophysical methods by Fechner. It provides a basis, in psychology, for the collection of *comparable* data, which is at the heart of the scientific method. More than 130 years later, Fechner's methods continue at the heart of psychophysics. Many of the data you will encounter as you navigate around *Exploring Perception* were gathered using the principles and methods he established. None of this is to say that psychology has not developed new and independent measures and methods (for example, reaction time studies and additive factor logic, multidimensional scaling, direct magnitude estimation, the preferential looking paradigm), but to underline the fundamental significance of Fechner's contribution.

Not only did Fechner provide a set of methods for the fledgling science of psychology, he provided a philosophical rationale that made sense of the data. It would be a mistake to assume that Fechner's contribution was limited to the study of sensation and perception. His methods and analyses have impacted on many other areas of the discipline—clinical psychology, social psychology, the study of personality, developmental psychology, and environmental psychology, for example.

The method of limits was given that name, not by Fechner, but by Emil Kraepelin, some 31 years after *Element der Psychophysik* was published. It was so-named because each stimulus series terminates when the limit—the point of change in judgment—is reached. It is important to understand why the method is crafted in the way it is. Before leaving Interaction 5.2.1, be sure that you understand what is meant by *errors of habituation* and *errors of anticipation* and know precisely how the method of limits avoids them.

A striking feature of the method of limits (and indeed the other psychophysical methods) is the fact that threshold varies from measurement to measurement, from series to series. It should not be surprising that threshold varies over time. Attention waivers, fatigue sets in, endogenous and exogenous distractions come and go, and background neural noise fluctuates. Sensation does not take place in a neural vacuum. The level of background sensations is constantly changing and so, accordingly, does the level of energy necessary to threshold detectability. To minimize threshold variability, a great deal of attention must be paid to the conditions under which observers are tested and the way in which a psychophysical experiment is conducted.

Exploring Perception provides you with many data-gathering tasks. Monitor yourself, the task, the environment, and your performance carefully. Be aware of extraneous factors that might influence your performance. Think how you might control them. Background noise might be a problem, for instance. It is not always possible to test subjects in a sound-attenuated room. Many experimenters have used random (white) noise to mask or obliterate unwanted auditory distractions. The essence of good psychophysics is care, careful observation of subjects and testing environment, attention to detail, and patience.

Be aware of the differences between the method of limits (Interaction 5.2.1) and the staircase methods (Interaction 5.2.3), and ensure that you understand why the latter represents a marked increase in efficiency. The staircase method is an example of what is called *adaptive testing*: the sequence of stimulus presentations is modified in the light of the observer's responses.

In Interaction 5.2.3, for example, the direction of intensity variation is changed each time the response changes: if, in the series of trials, Laszlo's response changes from *no* to *yes*—if the sound level exceeds threshold—sound intensity is immediately reduced on the next trial. If the response change is from *yes* to *no*—if the sound level falls below threshold—intensity is increased on the next trial. In this way, threshold is tracked. If sound intensity falls below threshold, it is immediately increased. If it moves above threshold in any series, intensity is immediately reduced. This is called a 1 up–1 down rule. Other rules (such as 1 up–3 down) are sometimes used, however, for a variety of statistical and methodological reasons.

The intensity steps in Interaction 5.2.3 were constant, but they too can be variable. In some experiments, step *size* is changed adaptively in the same way that step *direction* is changed. Subjects can be exposed to multiple, interleaved staircases in any series of trials. This can make prediction (anticipation) by the observer of what might happen next in the sequence of trials very difficult. The key point, here, is that the basic psychophysical methods are constantly being adapted and modified in the laboratory. Psychophysics is not a museum of ancient methods, but a field of vibrant change and adaptive innovation.

Be sure to note the differences between the variants of the method of limits used in Interactions 5.2.1 and 5.2.2. In the latter, which is concerned with estimating your difference threshold (rather than absolute threshold), you are permitted to judge a stimulus as "equal" to the standard. How does the impact on the method and the way in which threshold is calculated?

Unit 5.3 Signal Detection Theory

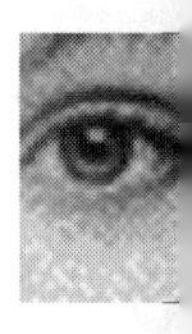

5.3.1 Probability Distributions
5.3.2 Evaluating Sensory Effects
5.3.3 Criterion and Kinds of Errors
5.3.4 Varying *d′* with Criterion Constant
5.3.5 Variables Affecting ROC Curves
5.3.6 ROC Curves, Criterion, and *d′*

The notion that there is a single, immutable, absolute threshold, which is a fundamental property of detection within a particular sensory system, has seemed increasingly unrealistic to psychophysicists. In fact, the concept of threshold, generally, has been marginalized in modern psychophysics. It is useful as a descriptor of capacity, or capability, but threshold or *limen* does not appear to be a useful general model of human detection of the presence or absence of a stimulus. It has no convenient way of dealing with the fluctuations in attention, motivation, strategy, sensitivity, demand, and criterion known to affect detection performance. It has no way of capturing its inherent variability, its demonstrably probabilistic quality. Moreover, the threshold model that permeates classical psychophysics has no way of modeling performance when there is no signal present to be detected. This is not a trivial issue: an observer can be correct or incorrect when making decisions when no signal is present; "false alarms," for example, can have important resource implications in (say) industrial, quality control, and defense settings.

It became clear to researchers that classical psychophysical approaches often yielded "biased" threshold estimates as observers' decision-making strategies interacted with their detection capability, particularly in the case of weak, marginal, or borderline stimulation. There was a clear need for bias-free estimates of observer sensitivity—which was what classical threshold methods were supposed to deliver, but never really had. The challenge was not to deny the clear "psychological" (or nonsensory) factors that impacted on detection performance, but to incorporate them into a truly general model of human detection performance. *Signal detection theory* (Green & Swets, 1966) begins to fulfill that role.

Signal detection theory, developed initially in electrical engineering to describe communication systems, is sometimes referred to in psychology as *sensory decision theory*. It is both a set of methods and a powerful psychophysical theory; it enables us to tease apart the sensory and nonsensory strands of detection performance. It provides a way of calculating independent indices of both the observer's sensory capacity and the criterion used in framing a decision. These may be thought of as the observer's ability to detect a stimulus and his or her response "bias" or "set," respectively

Signal detection theory assumes that all detection takes place against a background of eternally varying, random, neural *noise*. This noise is identical in *kind* to the activity generated by a signal, or stimulus, but different in sensory *extent* or *magnitude*. When present, a signal is superimposed on this noise.

Because the level of activity due to neural noise is random, it can have a high, medium, or low value at any instant, and it is assumed to be normally distributed, not least because of the elegant mathematical properties of the normal curve. Throughout this unit, the noise distribution is represented by the same bell-shaped curve with a standard deviation of 1. In essence, this noise distribution is the distribution of activation of the sensory system (channel) in the absence of a stimulus or signal.

When a signal is present, the activity due to it is simply added to the level of activation of the sensory system due to noise. We have, then, a second distribution of activity—the signal-plus-noise distribution—identical with the noise distribution but with a higher mean level of sensory activation.

This model recasts the detection task in an interesting and productive way. First, it takes into account the manifest variability in the sensory system. Second, the observer's task becomes to distinguish whether the experienced level of sensory activation is due to noise alone or to the presence of a signal in that noise—not that the observer conceives of the task in this way, however.

According to this model, the observer has to decide whether the experienced level of activation on a given trial is part of the noise distribution or the signal-plus-noise distribution. This would be relatively straightforward if the distributions didn't overlap—if there were a large difference between the means. This difference between the means indexes the discriminability or detectability of the signal—how well the observer can discriminate signal from noise. It is usually termed d' (pronounced *d-prime*). In general terms, the larger the value of d', the more detectable, or discriminable, the signal.

Logically, there are two ways d' can be increased: either by increasing the intensity (strength) of the signal, or by increasing the sensitivity of the observer. **Interaction 5.3.1** illustrates the equivalence of the influence of these two factors on d'. Both increase the mean of the signal-plus-noise distribution. Indeed, d' is conveniently indexed by the difference between the means of the two distributions (measured in units of the standard deviation of the distributions). Another way in which d' can be increased is by reducing the mean of the noise distribution.

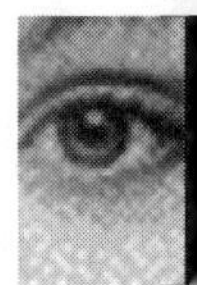

Spend some time on Interaction 5.3.1; the concepts developed there are pivotal to understanding the entire unit. Before moving on, be sure you understand what the probability distributions represent; why the noise and signal-plus-noise distributions are where they are on the sensory activation axis; and why varying signal intensity and observer sensitivity both impact on d'.

Whatever the relative location of the distributions and the difference between their means (d'), the observer must decide the level of activation above which he or she will report that a signal was present. In other words, the observer must set the criterion level of activation. Activation above that level will elicit a "yes, a signal is present" response, whereas activation below that level will elicit a "no," signal-absent, response. Logically, the criterion level of activation set is independent of the relative location of the distributions (indexed by d'): criterion and sensitivity are analytically separate—a major virtue of signal detection theory.

As you are probably aware by now, signal detection theory is a powerful, but rather abstract and difficult model. The interactions focus on how things change in a detection task and what this means for human performance. The emphasis is on helping you to *visualize,* in terms of the model, what these changes entail (i) for the relative location of the signal and signal-plus-noise distributions; (ii) for the extent of any overlap; (iii) for the location of the criterion level of activation; and, in turn (iv) for the patterns of error and correct responses that are observed.

For instance, in Interaction 5.3.1 you can vary an observer's sensitivity and the detectability of the stimulus independently, while monitoring what this means in terms of the underlying model. The key point to take away from this interaction is the fact that an increase in observer sensitivity and an increase in signal detectability are formally identical in terms of the model; both are reflected in a diminution of the overlap between the distributions—in an increase in the d' parameter of the model.

In **Interaction 5.3.2**, you can vary the level of sensory activation while holding the means of the noise and signal-plus-noise distributions constant. The idea, here, is that you monitor the probability that a given level of sensory activation is due to the presence of random noise alone, or to the presence of a signal embedded in noise. As you vary the level of sensory activation, keep an eye on the probability windows. Note, in particular, the region of overlap between the distributions, where errors can occur—where there is a finite likelihood that a given level of activation could be due to either the presence of a signal or to noise alone.

Interaction 5.3.3 is particularly important, insofar as it shows how to directly relate the model to actual performance on a given detection task. We can model an observer's behavior by assuming a criterion level of sensory activity, above which the observer responds, "Yes, a signal is present," and below which he or she reports no signal is present. This criterion will determine the number and types of errors made. A lax criterion, for instance, will result in many false alarms: the observer will report that a signal is present when none is.

The critical thing in this interaction is to make sure you can clearly distinguish definitionally between *hits, misses, correct rejections,* and *false alarms,* and that you can show how each class of response is defined by the relationship between the criterion (β) and the probability distributions. You should know what it means, for instance, to adopt a strict or a lax criterion and what the consequences of so doing will be for human performance. In experimental practice we reverse the logic, using the pattern of hits, misses, correct rejections, and false alarms in our data to estimate β and *d′*.

Interaction 5.3.4 enables you to vary *d′* with β constant and to monitor the consequences for performance in terms of the proportions of hits, misses, correct rejections, and false alarms. The important point, here, is to develop a feel for how *d′* and β together codetermine detection performance. That performance is elegantly summarized by plotting the percentage of hits against the percentage of false alarms for various experimental conditions or observers—establishing so-called *receiver operating characteristic* (or ROC) curves. **Interactions 5.3.5** and **5.3.6** introduce ROC curves. Be sure you understand why the shape of an ROC curve is affected by observer sensitivity and signal intensity, whereas varying signal probability affects the signal's location on a given ROC curve.

Unit 5.4 Information Theory

5.4.1 Generating Bits of Information
5.4.2 Odd Numbers of Alternatives
5.4.3 Binary Questions and Information
5.4.4 Information Transmission
5.4.5 Information and Event Probability
5.4.6 Channel Capacity

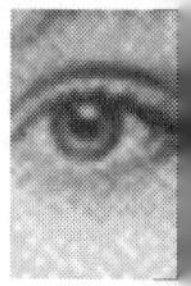

One of the central problems of psychophysics is *identification.* When studied experimentally, identification usually requires an observer to distinguish, and specify precisely, which item of a set of possible stimulus items has been presented on a given trial. The difficulty of such a task depends, among other things, on the number of items in the stimulus ensemble. Any index of the difficulty of an identification task must take this variable into account accordingly. *Information theory* provides just such an index.

Information theory, sometimes called communication theory, was developed initially (Shannon & Weaver, 1949) to describe the operation and efficiency of communications systems such as radio, telephone, and other forms of telecommunications. Part of a message transmitted in a noisy channel from source to destination, where it is decoded, could be lost. So, not all of the information sent was necessarily received and successfully decoded. Information could be lost, or distorted, due to noise, the complexity of the input, and/or inadequate channel capacity; the *fidelity* of the system could be less than perfect. There were virtues, clearly, in being able to specify precisely how much information was lost—or, conversely, successfully transmitted—in any telecommunications system.

Experimental psychologists, not least those involved in the study of sensation and perception, saw they had an analogous problem: The sensory system was not unlike a communication system—a stimulus might be thought of as input information; the output of the system might be equated with the psychologist's notion of response; and the ability of the system to process information seemed clearly related to its amount, complexity, and timing.

Information theory seemed to provide both a useful model and an elegant metric that might be used to better describe human sensory processing. A major virtue of the communication engineers' metric was that it was independent of the precise nature of the information being processed—that is, the detail of the stimulus array or input. In this sense, it had wide potential applicability to sensory psychology, in particular, and held out the promise—some would say a promise on which it failed to deliver—of a truly general theory of human performance.

Information was defined, in general terms, as being that which reduced a priori uncertainty. The amount of information generated by an event, or message, was defined so that it was equal to the reduction in uncertainty when it occurred. Before a coin is tossed, one is uncertain about what the outcome will be. When the event occurs, when the coin is tossed and comes to rest, the outcome is known; uncertainty is banished, and information has been generated. The unit of information—the binary digit, or *bit*—indeed was defined as the amount of information generated by the outcome of an event with two equiprobable alternatives (like the coin toss).

This meant it was possible to specify the information generated by an event precisely. If, in an item-recognition experiment, two stimuli were possible—A and B—and B was presented and recognized successfully by the subject, one bit of information was thus generated. If four stimuli—A, B, C, and D—were possible and C was successfully recognized, two bits of information were successfully processed, and so on. In general terms, the amount of information (H) generated by successful recognition is given by the formula: $H = \log_2 N$, where N is the number of equally likely stimulus alternatives. In this way, the information generated by successful recognition of one of eight equally likely stimulus alternatives is three bits. If there were sixteen alternatives, four bits of information would be generated, and so on.

The way in which the number of equiprobable alternative relates to the information processed/generated is illustrated in **Interactions 5.4.1** and **5.4.2**. You will probably find it useful to know the formula and be able to calculate the amount of information generated in any situation, at least those with equiprobable outcomes.

Another way of conceiving of information is in terms of the number of binary questions necessary to uniquely identify, or isolate, one of a defined set of equiprobable alternatives. With two items in the set, only one question would be necessary—for example: *Is it the item on the right?* One bit of information would be generated by the answer. With eight items, three questions would be necessary to identify the target. Three bits of information would be generated. Optimal repeated binary questions progressively rule out half the remaining alternatives—and therein lies their power, as anyone who has played Twenty Questions can attest! **Interaction 5.4.3** enables you to explore this principle in action. You would expect that any one of the set of eight objects can be uniquely identified with binary (yes/no) answers to three questions ($\log_2 8 = 3$). The computer identifies the target correctly every time—if you have been truthful in your answers!

So far, we have dealt with situations where information transmission was perfect, where human channel capacity was clearly adequate, and where the noise in the human (or computer) channel did not significantly affect performance. What would happen if, in the preceding item-recognition example, information transmission were less than perfect? Performance would become error-prone but, providing some information was transmitted, better than would be expected from chance alone. **Interaction 5.4.4** provides you with a simple simulation of letter-recognition performance under conditions of zero, moderate, and perfect information transmission. In that interaction, we are conceiving the subject as a human information-transmission channel, with the stimulus as channel input and the response as channel output. Note that data are summarized in a standard confusion matrix, which tabulates the response to each stimulus presented. Monitor closely how the contents of that matrix vary with transmission conditions.

So far, we have dealt with conditions under which all stimulus events were equiprobable. This is seldom the case in real-world situations outside casinos. The probability that the next car to come down the road will be a Chevrolet is not the same as the probability that it will be a Bugatti. It is not equally likely that you had raw seal for breakfast and cornflakes for breakfast. In **Interaction 5.4.5**, you can check how the information generated by an event varies as a function of its a priori probability. What you will quickly observe is that more information is generated by the occurrence of an unlikely event than by a likely one.

It is relatively simple to calculate the information generated by a particular outcome if all the possible outcomes are equiprobable; we simply take the logarithm to the base 2 of the number of alternative outcomes. As you will see in Interaction 5.4.5, hits to some part of the field are more probable than are hits to others, so the information generated by a given hit will be variable. Take care to note, in general terms, how the information generated by a hit relates to the relative frequencies shown:

$$H(x) = -\log p(x)$$

As discussed, and **as Interaction 5.4.6** illustrates, human observers can be regarded as information transmission channels. In fact, there is a relatively low limit on the amount of information that a human can transmit—in the vicinity of about 2.4 bits depending on the stimulus set (which corresponds to the approximate capacity of immediate memory, 7 ± 2 items). This low channel capacity sets a natural limit on, for instance, the number of tastes, smells, colors, or tones an observer can reliably identify, or discriminate, without some kind of cognitive reorganization or structuring.

Unit 5.5 Psychophysical Laws

5.5.1 Weber's Law
5.5.2 Weber's Law and the Weber Fraction
5.5.3 Weber's Law: Difference Thresholds
5.5.4 Fechner's Law
5.5.5 Stevens' Power Law
5.5.6 Cross-Modality Matching

Psychophysicists often have cause to estimate the minimum detectable difference between stimuli, called the *difference threshold*, *difference limen*, or *just noticeable difference*. They might want to establish, for example, the magnitude of the weight that is just noticeably different from a 200g standard weight; the length of a line that is just noticeably longer than a 1 meter standard; or the concentration of a solution that is just noticeably saltier than a 0.25mg/ml saline solution.

The difference threshold—the smallest just detectable difference between two stimuli—was introduced in Interactions 5.1.4 and 5.1.5, and some ways of estimating it have been explored (see, for example, Interaction 5.2.2). At base, it indicates just how different two stimuli must be to be seen to be different. You may be surprized to learn that Ernst Weber's seminal work on difference threshold actually predated Fechner's on absolute threshold. Fechner outlined Weber's contribution in his *Element der Psychophysik* (1860). Weber's basic work on difference threshold, the discrimination of relative differences, dates from about 1834.

Difference threshold studies usually involve comparisons between a standard stimulus, held constant, and comparison, or test, stimuli varied from trial to trial. It became clear from Weber's empirical studies that the just noticeable difference between two stimuli was not a constant, but depended critically on the magnitude of the standard stimulus. His initial work was on the difference threshold for lifted weights, where he had subjects compare a standard weight with comparison weights and judge which was heavier on each trial. He found that the difference threshold was proportional to the magnitude of the standard weight.

Weber repeated this estimation process for a range of judgments across the sense modalities. Within a sense modality and across a wide range of intensities, the ratio of the difference threshold to the standard stimulus was a constant. That constant was characteristic of the sense modality investigated. He expressed this relationship mathematically in what has become known as Weber's law: for any sense modality, the difference threshold (ΔI) varies as a function of the magnitude of the standard stimulus (I) multiplied by a constant (k). The constant, k, is characteristic of a given sense modality and is called the *Weber constant*, the *Weber fraction* or, occasionally, the *Weber ratio*. So, Weber's law is summarized by the equation $\Delta I = kI$.

Generally, the detection of a difference is relative to the intensity, or magnitude, of the standard. This principle makes intuitive sense. A teaspoon of sugar makes a discernible difference to the sweetness of a cup of coffee, but not to the sweetness of a vat of sugar syrup. The scent of a single rose can be detected in a living room, but probably not in a florist's shop full of them.

Interactions 5.5.1 to **5.5.3** provide you with a framework within which to explore how Weber's law works in various sense modalities. The mathematics is simple and worth mastering. Experiment with rearranging the equation. For instance, you can rearrange the expression of Weber's law to derive the Weber constant (k): $k = \Delta I/I$. The Weber constant indicates the proportion by which a standard stimulus must be changed to be detected by an observer 50% of the time. It is worth noting here that the difference threshold is not so much an immutable property, or attribute, of a sensory system, but simply a derived, operationalized, statistical measure.

As noted, there is a different Weber constant for each sensory continuum. The Weber constant for line length, for instance, is 0.029. Thus, for you to discriminate that a variable line is longer than a 100 cm standard line, the variable line must be at least 102.9 cm long.

You might find it easier to think of the change necessary to detection in *percentage* terms. The Weber constant for brightness is 0.079. This means that the intensity of a test stimulus must differ from the standard stimulus by 7.9% to be detectably different in brightness. Clearly, the greater the intensity of the standard (I), the larger 7.9% of it (ΔI) will be.

Generally, the smaller the Weber constant, the more sensitive is the sensory system in question. A sense modality with a small Weber constant will be able to detect a small difference in magnitude or intensity. The Weber constant for brightness is relatively large. As we have seen, it takes a 7.9% change to detect a difference in brightness. By comparison, it requires only a 2.9% change in the length of a line to provide a just noticeable difference (Weber constant: 0.029).

It is useful to be precise about the difference between the difference threshold (ΔI) and the just noticeable difference. The terms tend to be used more or less interchangeably, although they are not synonymous. Be aware that, whereas the threshold is measured in physical units (intensity, length, weight), the just noticeable difference refers to psychological experience; it is a unit of subjective sensory intensity or magnitude. Strictly, the difference threshold is the physical change necessary to produce a just noticeable difference; it is important that you keep this distinction in mind.

The measurement of just noticeable differences can be made by any of the classical psychophysical methods outlined in Unit 5.2—the method of limits, the method of constant stimuli, and the method of adjustment. It is worth spending a little time working out how you would adapt each method to do those measurements.

Gustav Fechner's massive methodological contribution to psychophysics was outlined in the discussion of Unit 5.1. He also set up its theoretical-philosophical scaffolding. It is difficult to overstate the importance of his precept that sensory experience is *quantitatively* related to properties of the physical stimulus. This is the central premise on which psychophysics is founded; Fechner held out the prospect of a nontrivial quantification of mind. It begs the question, of course, as to the precise quantitative nature of that relationship. Fechner, in addition to his methodological and theoretical contribution, addressed this empirical issue directly. In so doing, he built on Weber's earlier work, taking as his starting point the idea that ΔI—or, more accurately, the just noticeable difference produced by a change of ΔI—could be used as a metric for the subjective magnitude of a sensation. He proposed the use of the just noticeable difference as the unit of measurement for sensations. This made it possible to express elegantly the subjective, or psychological, magnitude of sensations as a function of physical stimulus magnitude.

Fechner's use of the just noticeable difference, a psychological constant, as the unit of measurement had a pivotal virtue: the difference between two stimuli separated by a just noticeable difference was the same, irrespective of the actual value of the stimuli. In contrast (as Weber's law makes clear), ΔI increases with stimulus magnitude; it is not a constant.

Fechner formalized the relationship between sensed magnitude (expressed in just noticeable differences) and physical magnitude: the former increases *arithmetically* as the latter increases *geometrically*. In essence, the relationship between them is *logarithmic*. Fechner's log law expresses this: $S = c \bullet \log(I)$, where sensation (S) is proportional to the log of stimulus magnitude (I) and c is a constant of proportionality related to Weber's constant (**Interaction 5.5.4**).

Almost 100 years elapsed before S. S. Stevens formulated a more accurate mathematical description of the relationship between sensed and physical intensity (**Interaction 5.5.5**). Stevens demonstrated that the relationship was better described by a power function than a log function: $P = kS^n$, where P is perceived magnitude, k is a constant, and S is the stimulus intensity raised to the power n. In Stevens' power law, it is the exponent, n, that is characteristic of the given sensory modality. Each modality, then, has a distinctive, empirically derived (measured) exponent, which relates sensed and physical intensity.

Stevens made considerable empirical use of direct magnitude estimation when developing his stimulus-sensation curves: subjects simply ascribed numbers (relative magnitudes) to their perceptual experience. You can explore how direct magnitude estimation works in Unit 5.6 (Interaction 5.6.5). This approach was criticized on the grounds that it arguably tells us more about how humans use numbers than the magnitude of sensory experience per se. To counter this argument, Stevens developed a scaling technique called *cross-modality matching*—illustrated in **Interaction 5.5.6**—in which numbers were not used at all.

Human observers are able to map one sense modality onto another. For instance, they can adjust a light to make it as bright as the pitch of a sound is high, or adjust water temperature so that it feels as hot as a light is bright. This capacity is at the heart of Stevens' cross-modality matching. Generally, subjects adjust the intensity of a stimulus until it matches the intensity of a stimulus from a second sensory continuum: they match sensory intensities across sensory modalities. Despite the fact that subjects do not, as such, assign numbers to experience, the data still are well described by the power law. We have included cross-modality matching in this unit because it is generally held to provide the soundest basis, the most appropriate modern methodology, for the measurement of the sensory magnitudes that so-beguiled Gustav Fechner and, much later, S. S. Stevens.

Unit 5.6 Psychophysical Scaling

5.6.1 Attributes of Scales
5.6.2 More Examples of Scales
5.6.3 Assign Variables to Scales
5.6.4 Scales, Data, and Statistics
5.6.5 Direct Magnitude Estimation
5.6.6 Prothetic and Metathetic Continua

A quantitative psychology clearly requires that we first assign numbers to events observed in the seamless ebb and flow of human behavior. Once numbers are assigned to events, we are able to manipulate them symbolically and arithmetically and to compare and contrast them with varying degrees of precision. A scale assigns numbers to observed events and, in so doing, renders those events more amenable to scientific investigation and analysis.

This unit and Unit 5.8 examine four classes of scales in some depth: *nominal*, *ordinal*, *interval*, and *ratio* scales. Nominal scales do no more than place objects or events in mutually exclusive categories. They tell us nothing of the nature and extent of the differences between them. We can do no more than count the number of items within a category. Thus, the diagnostic categories "measles," "mumps," and "whooping cough" can be thought of as lying on a nominal scale. It is possible, of course, to count the number of cases of each illness in a population, but this will tell us nothing of the relative severity of the cases within a category, or the relationships between the various classes of disease. With nominal scales, we know no more than that the categories are analytically distinct. Any exercise in taxonomic classification (in, say, botany or biology) amounts to assigning cases to categories on a nominal scale.

Like nominal scales, ordinal scales assign names to objects or events, but they also tell us about the *properties* of those things. An ordinal scale permits distinctions to be drawn between things along some observable dimension. When we arrange materials according to their hardness, oranges according to their sweetness, or people according to their passivity, we are assigning them to an ordinal scale.

It is possible to describe the properties of things on an ordinal scale in relative terms; they can have more or less of an attribute. However, although we note that Pete Sampras ranks number 1 in the tennis world and Andre Agassi ranks 5, we do not know that the difference in skill between them is the same as that between the players ranking 25 and 30, respectively. In other words, we have no assurance that the intervals on an ordinal scale are equal. So, the Association of Tennis Professionals (ATP) rankings constitute an ordinal scale.

Ordinal scales can provide useful information, but it is of limited precision. This shortcoming is less important when making gross distinctions. So, it is accurate and meaningful to say that pugilists are more overtly aggressive, on average, than Buddhist monks; but it is difficult to precisely quantify that aggression and compare it with the difference in the overt aggressiveness between baseball players and ballerinas. In this sense, ordinal scales index *differences*, but provide no precise information as to the magnitude of those differences.

Like nominal and ordinal scales, interval scales assign names to objects or things. They are more precise, however. Unlike ordinal scales, the intervals on interval scales are equal; there is a constant difference between scale values. Temperature, for instance, is an interval scale. The difference in temperature between 35 degrees and 37 degrees is precisely that between 16 degrees and 18 degrees. Because all the intervals on an interval scale are equal, interval scales allow precise quantification of the differences between things.

The zero point on an interval scale is entirely arbitrary; it is no more than a convenient starting point for the scale. It does not correspond to a total absence of the attribute being measured. For example, the 0 degrees Fahrenheit on a thermometer does not denote a total absence of heat.

Ratio scales—the most sophisticated mode of measurement—not only have all the properties of the other scales, they have an absolute zero point as well. Not surprising perhaps is that ratio scales are encountered more in the physical than in the psychological domain: the ratio scales "height," "weight," "time," and "length," for instance, all have an absolute zero point. Ratio scales are amenable to the full spectrum range of mathematical operations and, accordingly, lend themselves to sophisticated mathematical manipulation. It makes sense to say that one person lost three times as much weight as another—because weight is a ratio scale—but it does not make sense to say that an analgesic can reduce pain by half. Pain cannot be measured on a ratio scale.

Remember, scales serve to quantify (to assign numbers to) objects, experiences, or events to make them amenable to mathematical manipulation and analysis. Accordingly, scaling is a very important part of psychology's armory of methods, and it has developed a wide range of techniques for developing, or deriving, different kinds of scales. You will have the opportunity to experience many of these methods as you work through this unit and, in particular, Unit 5.8. It is important that you understand the logic of those methods and how they achieve the ends they do. They are discussed in more detail in the Unit 5.8 guide.

Not all sensory qualities can be scaled in the same way. Some objects have attributes that can be easily quantified and some do not. It is easy to assign meaningful numbers that describe, for example "how much" height or weight an object possesses. Such sensory qualities are said to lie on *prothetic* continua. If we add height, an object gets "higher": changes in the physical stimulus give rise to changes in the apparent quantity of the stimulus. Other changes in a sensory stimulus give rise to changes in *type* or *quality*. In those cases, it makes sense not to ask *how much* of an attribute there is, but *what kind* it is. These attributes are said to lie on *metathetic* continua. In studies of perception, it is often useful to distinguish between prothetic and metathetic variables.

As **Interaction 5.6.6** makes clear, prothetic variables are those where a larger value implies a greater quantity. A metathetic variable, on the other hand, is qualitative in nature. Eye color, for instance, is a metathetic variable. There are no quantitative differences between eye colors. Whereas prothetic variables can be measured with virtually any kinds of scales, metathetic variables can be measured only with nominal scales. The distinction is introduced in Interaction 5.6.6, by distinguishing more clearly between quantitative and qualitative variables—that is, between those variables to which meaningful numbers can be applied and normal arithmetic operations carried out, and those which can simply be named or categorized (then counted perhaps).

Unit 5.7 Context and Perceptual Experience

5.7.1 Context: The Titchener Illusion
5.7.2 Context: The Delboeuf Illusion
5.7.3 Context: The Judd Illusion
5.7.4 Context: The Ponzo Illusion
5.7.5 Context: Brightness Assimilation
5.7.6 Context and Apparent Length

The relationship between sensed and physical magnitudes—the core problem of psychophysics—is seldom straightforward. Perception of size, magnitude, and intensity, for example, is not always accurate; it does not take place in a vacuum. The context in which a *focal* stimulus (the stimulus that is the center of attention) is set can profoundly affect the way in which it is perceived.

Our sensory-perceptual systems are particularly vulnerable to perturbation and distortion by temporally and/or spatially contiguous stimuli. Context would not be a particular problem if perception were ultimately analytic rather than synthetic. But humans tend to see perceptual "wholes" (*Gestalten*) rather than their "parts." The total stimulus array—including strictly nonrelevant contextual elements or events—is an integral part of most perceptual experience.

This is not to say that humans are not capable of focusing attention, or of selectively processing part of an array, but rather that they tend to process information globally. In the first instance, the stimulus array is processed *in toto*, as a matter of implicit habit, unconscious "strategy," or hardwired neurophysiological predisposition. It is often possible, of course, to filter out irrelevant background or contextual features, with controlled, conscious effort. Sometimes it is not.

Stimulus context—the apparently nonrelevant, background elements in a perceptual field—can induce a variety of perceptual distortions, misperceptions, or illusions. The reasons why they do are usually not clear. Even the simplest illusions have long histories of theoretical controversy (see the discussion of Unit 4.3, for example).

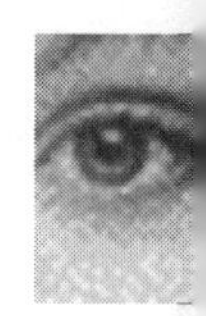

It seems highly likely that many size illusions derive from misplaced, or inappropriate, size-distance scaling. Perceptual context, in that case, seems to provide misleading cues as to the relative depth of some elements, at least, in the perceptual field. The illusions investigated in **Interactions 5.7.1** to **5.7.4**, for example, arguably derive from this source. Those interactions enable you to explore directly the effect of context on your perceptions, on your psychophysical judgments.

It is likely that you will have seen versions of some, or all, of the illusions in this unit before. What is different, here, is that you can quantify their effects; try consciously filtering out the contextual elements that appear to induce them, then reestimate the effect of the illusion; and, ultimately, delete those inducing elements entirely. The crucial point, for our purposes, is that perceptual judgments can be markedly influenced by contextual fields, both in the psychophysics laboratory and in a variety of everyday situations. Perception is an active, constructive process, and a variety of external and internal factors can impinge on it.

These contextual effects go far beyond distortions of size and magnitude, of course: shape, color, orientation, and brightness are just some of the stimulus attributes or properties that can be misperceived. *Temporal* context can be as important, in this sense, as *spatial* context. Not only is perception of a stimulus affected by it surroundings, but also by preceding and subsequent events.

There are a great many other examples of contextual effects throughout *Exploring Perception*, for example: simultaneous color contrast (Interaction 3.8.5); simultaneous brightness contrast (Interaction 4.8.4); illusory contours (Unit 2.3); figural, tilt, and shape aftereffects (Interactions 2.4.1 to 2.4.3); contextual and field effects in apparent movement (Unit 2.6); induced movement (Interaction 2.7.3); waterfall and spiral motion aftereffects (Interactions 2.7.5 and 2.7.6); moving phantom gratings (Interaction 2.8.2); context and apparent speed (Interaction 2.8.4); velocity transposition (Interaction 2.8.5); causality and the launching effect (Interaction 2.8.6); and a wide variety of size-distance and other illusions (Unit 4.3).

What should become abundantly clear as you work through these interactions, and others, is that perception of a stimulus is fundamentally *relative* in nature and is mediated not only by its absolute, intrinsic properties, but by the comparative relations between that stimulus and the spatio-temporal context in which it is set.

There have been various attempts to explain the effect of context on sensed magnitude. One of the more durable and plausible is that advanced by Helson (1964). In general terms, he suggests that the organism accommodates itself to the environment by establishing an internal standard—a *reference level* or *adaptation level*—against which all environmental stimuli are judged. In this sense, *all* judgments are relative. According to *adaptation level theory*, sensory stimuli are not simply larger or smaller in their own right, but they are larger or smaller by comparison with the internal psychological (subjective) adaptation level, which tends to exacerbate differences to the extent that it reinforces them. Adaptation level plays a role, then, in sensed magnitude or perceptual intensity, complicating the relationship between sensed and physical magnitudes, which is the primary concern of psychophysics.

Context plays a pivotal role in motion perception, for instance. Perceived velocity, direction of movement, trajectory of movement, and the perception of causation are all markedly affected by features of the perceptual field in which they occur. Indeed, the threshold for movement detection can be dramatically lower in a patterned field than in a homogeneous one.

As we saw in the discussion of Units 2.5 to 2.8, the perceived velocity of a moving stimulus depends not only on its rate of displacement, but on the context (or frame of reference) in which that movement is taking place. For instance, the size of the field in which an object is moving can markedly affect its apparent velocity, as Interaction 2.8.3 clearly demonstrates. The smaller the field of movement, the greater the apparent velocity of a moving object.

As we saw in Unit 2.8, contextual factors other than field size also can play an important role in determining apparent velocity. For instance, in Interaction 2.8.4, the apparent speed of the constant-speed soccer ball increases as it approaches either end of the reference box in which it moves. This interaction is an analog of an early study by Brown (1931). He showed that a small object was also speeded as it approached and crossed under a central fixation string.

The phenomenon of *velocity transposition* is a striking example of contextual effects on movement perception. As you can see demonstrated in Interaction 2.8.3, a large object moving in a large window, or context, appears to move more slowly than a small object moving in a small window. In this sense, a cat in a large cage must move faster than a mouse in a small cage to be seen to be moving at the same speed. There is a clear interaction between stimulus and context.

Not only does the frame of reference affect the apparent velocity of objects, it is a vital factor in determining motion detection thresholds. Contextual effects have been shown to influence judgments of sensory magnitude even when the context is in a different sense modality from the stimulus being judged (for an example, see Coren et al., 1993, Box 2-6, p. 58).

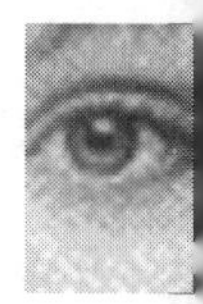

Unit 5.8 Constructing Psychophysical Scales

5.8.5 Method of Category Production
5.8.6 Response Compression and Expansion

Unit 5.6 provides an introduction to psychological scaling and is designed to facilitate your exploration of the attributes of nominal, ordinal, interval and ratio scales. It provides a number of examples of types of scales (Interactions 5.6.1, 5.6.2, and 5.6.3) and encourages you to think in depth about the type of statistical techniques appropriate to each (Interaction 5.6.4). With the exception of Interaction 5.6.5, which deals with direct magnitude estimation as a tool for generating scales, Unit 5.6 does not go into the detail of how scales are constructed. You are able to explore several methods for the derivation of scales, however, in this final unit, Unit 5.8.

Interaction 5.8.1 provides an overview of scaling methods. You might find it preferable to work quickly through this interaction at first—building a kind of loose conceptual scaffolding—then return to it, either from time to time or at the completion of the unit, to consolidate and organize what you know.

Interactions 5.8.2 through **5.8.5** are intended to acquaint you with, and to give you experience using, some commonly used scaling techniques. In each case, you are invited to make a series of judgments and register a set of responses. At the end of each task, the program calculates and displays the scale implicitly defined by your judgments. As previously hinted at, you might find it useful to return to Interaction 5.8.1 from time to time to check the logic and detail of each method and, in particular, the way in which the scale is calculated in each case.

The scales all address a common end: they are attempts to represent numerically and graphically a specified psychological property, or quality, of objects or events. It may help to keep in mind the distinction between prothetic and metathetic continua, encountered in Interaction 5.6.6, when working through this unit. All of the scaling exercises in Unit 5.8 deal with variables that lie on one of these two types of continua. Be sure you know which one. Remember, metathetic continua must be measured only with *nominal* scales.

It is worth noting that the powerful contextual effects explored in Unit 5.7 have been shown to influence a wide variety of psychological scaling methods, including cross-modality matching (Interaction 5.5.6); direct magnitude estimation (Interaction 5.6.5); and category estimation (Interaction 5.8.4). This begs the question whether these contextual effects are influencing merely the response one gives or the actual process of perception. In the language of signal detection theory (see

Unit 5.3), do contextual effects influence β or *d′*? Evidence suggests that *both* may be influenced by spatially and/or temporally contiguous events (Algom & Marks, 1990; Schneider & Parker, 1990).

In psychophysics, sensed magnitude can sometimes increase more slowly than increases in physical intensity, as is the case with brightness. Increases in intensity bring forth smaller increases in brightness, an effect exacerbated at higher intensities—as is strikingly obvious in Interaction 4.6.2. This is the phenomenon of *response compression*. Sometimes, psychological magnitude increases more rapidly than physical magnitude—the phenomenon of *response expansion*. Electric shock is a case in point. Occasionally, the function relating these two variables is linear with unit slope, as is the case with judgments of line length—sensed and physical magnitude increase at the same rate.

You can explore both response compression and response expansion in **Interaction 5.8.6.** It is possible to express these relationships in terms of the exponent (n) in Stevens' power functions (see Interaction 5.5.5): $P = kS^n$. The exponent for judgments of line length is 1.0, the exponent for brightness judgments is 0.33, and that for electric shock is 3.5. Thus, response compression is indexed by an exponent less than 1.0 (the power function relating sensed magnitude to stimulus intensity curves downward), whereas response expansion is indexed by an exponent more than 1.0 (the power function curves upward).

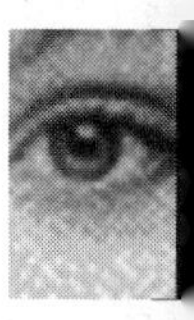

Credits for Interactions

Module 1 *Physiological Bases of Perception*

1.1.2 Adapted from Graham (1990)/*1.1.5* Adapted from Graham (1990)/*1.1.6* Photo by Fritz Goro /*1.2.4* Adapted from Graham (1990)/*1.3.4* Adapted from Goldstein (1989, Fig. 2-13)/*1.4.4* Adapted from Kalat (1995, Fig. 3.8)/*1.4.5* Based on Graham (1990, pp.140–145)/*1.5.1* Adapted from Ratliff (1965)/*1.5.2* Adapted from Kalat (1995)/*1.5.3* Adapted from Goldstein (1996, Figs. 2.29–2.31)/*1.5.5* Adapted from Goldstein (1989)/*1.5.6* Based on Hartline (1940) & Kuffler (1953)/*1.6.1* Adapted from Hubel & Wiesel (1961)/*1.6.3* Based on Sekuler & Blake (1994, Figs. 3.6 & 3.7)/*1.6.4* Adapted from Hubel & Wiesel (1959)/*1.6.5* Adapted from Hubel & Wiesel (1959)/*1.6.6* Adapted from Hubel & Wiesel (1965)/*1.7.2* Adapted from Lindsay & Norman (1977)/*1.8.2* Adapted from Spear, Penrod, & Baker (1988) & Schiffman (1990, Fig. 10.5)/*1.8.5* Adapted from Culler, Coakley, Lowy, & Gross (1943)/*1.8.6* Adapted from Wever (1949).

Module 2 *Form, Pattern, and Movement*

2.1.5 From Matlin (1992, Fig. 5.8c) & Benjamin, Hopkins, & Nation (1994, Fig. 4-5)/*2.2.1* *Pintos* by Bev Doolittle (1979)/*2.2.2* Kaiser Porcelain Limited, London/*2.2.4* From Hochberg (1971)/*2.2.5* Adapted from Klymenko & Weisstein (1986)/*2.3.2* Based on Schiffman (1990, Fig 14.34)/*2.3.3* Based on Schiffman (1990, Fig 14.34)/*2.3.4* From Kanizsa (1979)/*2.3.5* Based on Ehrenstein (1941)/*2.4.1* After Köhler & Wallach (1944)/*2.4.2* Based on Gibson & Radner (1937)/*2.4.5* From Coren, Ward, & Enns (1994, Fig. 11-12)/*2.4.6* From Coren, Ward, & Enns (1994, Fig. 11-12)/*2.5.4* Based on Kolers (1972)/*2.5.6* Based on Kolers & von Grunau (1976) & Kolers & Pomerantz (1971)/*2.6.1* Based on Shepard & Zare (1983)/*2.6.2* Based on Kolers (1972)/*2.6.3* Based on Wertheimer (1912)/*2.6.5* Based on Ramachandran & Anstis (1986)/*2.7.1* Based on Ternus (1926)/*2.7.2* Based on Ramachandran, Rao, & Vidyasagar (1973)/*2.7.4* Based on Ramachandran & Anstis (1986)/*2.8.1* Based on Festinger & Easton (1974)/*2.8.2* From Tynan & Sekuler (1975)/*2.8.3* Based on Brown (1931)/*2.8.4* Based on Brown (1931)/*2.8.5* Based on Brown (1931).

Module 3 *Perceiving Color*

3.1.4 Adapted from Clulow (1972) & Goldstein (1996, Figs. 4-5 & 4-6)/*3.3.1* Based on Wald & Brown (1965)/*3.3.2* Based on Wald & Brown (1965)/*3.3.3* Based on Wald & Brown (1965)/*3.3.4* Based on Wald & Brown (1965)/*3.4.3* From Gray (1994, Fig. 8.18)/*3.4.4* Adapted from Coren, Ward, & Enns (1994)/ *3.4.6* Adapted from Wright (1929)/*3.5.3* Based on Hurvich & Jameson (1957) & adapted from Goldstein (1989, Fig 4-15)/*3.5.4* Based on Hurvich & Jameson (1957) & adapted from Goldstein (1989, Fig. 4-16)/*3.5.5* Based on Hurvich & Jameson (1957) & adapted from Goldstein (1989, Fig. 4-17)/*3.6.5* Based on Wald & Brown (1965)/*3.7.6* Photo by Craig McClain, construction by Floyd Fronius, after a concept by Vladamir Chaika.

Module 4 *Depth, Size, Brightness, and Contrast*

4.1.1 Jeff Hunter/The Image Bank/*4.1.2* Jaime Budge/Windskate, Inc./*4.1.3* Based on Ramachandran (1988)/*4.3.1* From Goldstein (1996, Fig. 6-42)/*4.4.6* Based on Levine & Shefner (1991, Fig. 12-17)/*4.5.2* Based on Wallach & O'Connell (1953)/*4.5.5* Adapted from Rogers & Graham (1979)/*4.6.1* Adapted from Rushton (1961)/*4.7.6* Based on Levine & Shefner (1991, Fig. 10-6)/*4.8.2* From Blakemore & Sutton (1969, p. 245)/*4.8.3* Adapted from Goldstein (1989, Figs. 5.29, 5.30, & 5.31)/*4.8.5* Based on Burton, Nagshineh, & Ruddock, (1977).

Module 5 *Psychophysics*

5.4.6 From Coren, Ward, & Enns (1994, Fig. 2.9)/*5.7.5* From Festinger, Coren, & Rivers (1970) & illustrated in Coren, Ward, & Enns (1994, Fig. 4-22).

References

Algom, D., & Marks, L. E. (1990). Range and regression, loudness scales, and loudness processing: Toward a context-bound psychophysics. *Journal of Experimental Psychology: Human Perception and Performance, 16*, 706–727.

Berbaum, K., Tharp, D., & Mroczek, K. (1983). Depth perception of surfaces in pictures: Looking for conventions of depiction in Pandora's box. *Perception, 12*, 5–20.

Benjamin, L. T., Hopkins, J. R., & Nation, J. R. (1992). *Sensation and Perception* (2nd ed.). New York: Macmillan

Blakemore, C., & Sutton, P. (1969). Size adaptation: A new aftereffect. *Science, 166*, 245–247.

Bowmaker, J. K., & Dartnell, H. J. A. (1980). Visual pigments of rods and cones in the human retina. *Journal of Physiology, 298*, 501–511.

Bradley, D. R., & Dumais, S. T. (1975). Ambiguous cognitive contours. *Nature, 257*, 582–584.

Bradley, D. R., & Petry, H. M. (1977). Organizational determinants of subjective contour: The subjective Necker cube. *American Journal of Psychology, 90*, 253–262.

Brown, P. K., & Wald, G. (1964). Visual pigments in single rods and cones in the human retina. *Science, 144*, 45–52.

Brown, J. F. (1931). The thresholds for visual movement. *Psychologische Forschung, 14*, 249–268. Reprinted in I. M. Spigel (Ed.*)*, Readings in the study of visually perceived movement. New York: Harper & Row, 1965.

Brown, J. F. (1931b). The visual perception of velocity. *Psychologische Forschung*, 14, 199–232. Reprinted in I. M. Spigel (Ed.), Readings in the study of visually perceived movement. New York: Harper & Row, 1965.

Buchsbaum, G., & Gottschalk, A. (1983). Trichromacy, opponent colours coding, and the optimum colour information in the retina. *Proceedings of the Royal Society of London*, Series B, *220*, 89–113.

Burton, G. J., Nagshineh, S., & Ruddock, K. H. (1977). Processing by the human visual system of the light and dark contrast components of the retinal image. *Biological Cybernetics, 27*, 189–197.

Chapanis, A., & Mankin, D. A. (1967). The horizontal-vertical illusion in a visually rich environment. *Perception & Psychophysics, 2*, 249–255.

Clulow, F. W. (1972). *Color: Its principles and their application.* New York: Morgan & Morgan.

Coren, S. (1972). Subjective contours and apparent depth. *Psychological Review, 79*, 359–367.

Coren, S., & Girgus, J. S. (1978). *Seeing is deceiving: The psychology of visual illusion.* Hillsdale, NJ: Lawrence Erlbaum.

Coren, S., & Girgus, J. S. (1980). Principles of perceptual organization: The Gestalt illusions. *Journal of Experimental Psychology: Human Perception and Performance, 6*, 404–412.

Coren, S., Ward, L. M., & Enns, J. T. (1994). *Sensation and perception* (4th ed.). Orlando, FL: Harcourt Brace.

Cornsweet, T. N. (1962). The staircase method in psychophysics. *American Journal of Psychology, 75*, 485–91.

Culler, E. A., Coakley, J. D., Lowy, K., & Goss, N. (1943). A revised frequency-map of the guinea-pig cochlea. *American Journal of Psychology, 56*, 475–500.

DeLucia, P. R., & Hochberg, J. (1985). Illusions in the real world and in the mind's eye (Abstract). *Proceedings of the Eastern Psychological Association, 56*, 38.

DeLucia, P. R., & Hochberg, J. (1986). Real-world geometrical illusions: Theoretical and practical implications (Abstract). *Proceedings of the Eastern Psychological Association, 57*, 62.

DeLucia, P. R., & Hochberg, J. (1991). Geometrical illusions in solid objects under ordinary viewing conditions. *Perception and Psychophysics, 50*, 547–554.

Derrington, A. M., Lennie, P., & Krauskopf, J. (1983). Chromatic response properties of parvocellular neurons in the macaque LGN. In J. D. Mollon & L. T. Sharpe (Eds.), *Color vision* (pp. 245–251). London: Academic Press.

Devalois, R. L., & DeValois, K. K. (1980). Spatial vision. *Annual Review of Psychology, 31*, 309–341.

Devalois, R. L., & Jacobs, G. H. (1984). Neural mechanisms of color vision. In J. M. Brookhart & V. B. Mountcastle (Eds.), *Handbook of physiology: 3. The nervous system.* Bethesda, MD: American Psychological Society.

Dumais, S. T., & Bradley, D. R. (1976). The effects of illumination level and retinal size on the apparent strength of subjective contours. *Perception & Psychophysics, 19*, 339–345.

Ehrenstein, W. (1941). Concerning variations in L. Hermann's brightness observations. *Zeitschrift fur Psychologie*, 150, 83–91.

Enns, J. T., & Girgus, J. S. (1985). Perceptual grouping and spatial distortion: A developmental study. *Developmental Psychology, 21*, 241–246.

Fechner, G. T. (1860). *Element der psychophysik.* Leipzig: Breitkopf & Harterl.

Festinger, L., Coren, S., & Rivers, G. (1970). The effect of attention on brightness contrast and assimilation. *American Journal of Psychology*, 83, 189–207.

Festinger, L., & Easton, A. M. (1974). Inferences about the efferent system based on a perceptual illusion produced by eye-movements. *Psychological Review, 18,* 44–58.

Frisby, J. P. (1980). *Seeing.* New York: Oxford University Press.

Frisby, J. P., & Clatworthy, J. L. (1975). Illusory contours: Curious cases of simultaneous brightness contrast? *Perception, 4,* 349–357.

Gibson, J. J., & Radner, M. (1937). Adaptation, aftereffect, and contrast in the perception of tilted lines. I. Quantitative studies. *Journal of Experimental Psychology,* 20, 453–467.

Gillam, B. (1971). A depth processing theory of the Poggendorff illusion. *Perception & Psychophysics, 10,* 211–216.

Gillam, B. (1980). Geometrical illusions. *Scientific American, 242,* 102–111.

Goldstein, E. B. (1989). *Sensation and perception* (3rd ed.). Pacific Grove, CA: Brooks/Cole.

Goldstein, E. B. (1996). *Sensation and perception* (4th ed.). Pacific Grove, CA: Brooks/Cole.

Graham, R. B. (1990). *Physiological psychology.* Belmont, CA: Wadsworth.

Gray, P. (1994). *Psychology* (2nd ed.). New York: Worth.

Green, D. M., & Swets, J. A. (1966*). Signal detection theory and psychophysics.* New York: John Wiley & Sons.

Hartline, H. K. (1940). The receptive fields of optic nerve fibers. *American Journal of Physiology, 130,* 690–699.

Helson, H. (1964). *Adaptation-level theory.* New York: Harper & Row.

Hochberg, J. E. (1971). Perception in J. W. Kling & L. A. Riggs (Eds.) *Experimental Psychology* (3rd ed., pp. 396–550). New York: Holt, Rinehart, & Winston.

Hubel, D. H., & Livingstone, M. S. (1990). Color puzzles. *Cold Spring Harbor Symposia on Quantitative Biology, 60,* 643–649.

Hubel, D. H., & Wiesel, T. N. (1959). Receptive fields of single neurons in the cat's striate cortex. *Journal of Physiology, 148,* 574–591.

Hubel, D. H., & Wiesel, T. N. (1961). Integrative action in the cat's lateral geniculate body. *Journal of Physiology, 155,* 385–398.

Hubel, D. H., & Wiesel, T. N. (1965). Receptive fields and functional architecture in two non-striate visual areas (18 and 19) of the cat. *Journal of Neurophysiology, 28,* 229–289.

Hurvich, L. M., & Jameson, D. (1957). An opponent-process theory of color vision. *Psychological Review, 64,* 384–404.

Jory, M. K., & Day, R. H. (1979). The relationship between brightness contrasts and subjective contours. *Perception, 8,* 3–9.

Julesz, B., & Bergen, J. R. (1983). Textons, the fundamental elements in preattentive vision and perception of contours. *The Bell System Technical Journal, 62*(6), 1619–1645.

Kalat, J. W. (1995). *Biological psychology* (5th ed.). Pacific Grove, CA: Brooks/Cole.

Kanizsa, G. (1979). *Organization in vision: Essays on Gestalt perception.* New York: Praeger.

Klymenko, V., & Weisstein, N. (1986). Spatial frequency differences can determine figure–ground organization. *Journal of Experimental Psychology: Human Perception and Performance, 12*, 324–330.

Köhler, W., & Wallach, H. (1944). Figural aftereffects: An investigation of visual processes. *Proceedings of the American Philosophical Society, 88*, 269–357.

Kolers, P. A., and von Grunau, M. (1976). Shape and color in apparent motion. *Vision Research, 16*, 329–335.

Kolers, P. A., & Pomerantz, J. R. (1971). Figural change in apparent motion. *Journal of Experimental Psychology*, 87, 99–108.

Levine, M. W., & Shefner, J. M. (1991). *Fundamentals of sensation and perception* (2nd ed.). Pacific Grove, CA: Brooks/Cole.

Lindsay, P. H., & Norman, D. A. (1977). *Human information processing: An introduction to psychology.* New York: Academic Press.

Marks, W. B., Dobelle, W. H., & MacNichol, E. F. (1964). Visual pigments of single primate cones. *Science, 143*, 1181–1183.

Matlin, M. W. (1992). *Psychology.* Fort Worth: Harcourt Brace Jovanovich.

Matlin, M. W., & Foley, H. J. (1992). *Sensation and Perception* (3rd ed.). Needham Heights, MA: Allyn and Bacon.

Müller, J. (1842). *Elements of physiology* (W. Baly, Trans.). London: Taylor & Walton.

Murch, G. M. (1976). Classical conditioning of the McCollough effect: Temporal parameters. *Vision Research, 16*, 615–619.

Pantle, A., & Picciano, L. (1976). A multistable movement display: Evidence for two separate movement systems in human vision. *Science, 193*, 500–502.

Pollack, R. H., & Jaeger, T. B. (1991). The effect of lightness contrast on the colored Müller-Lyer illusion, *Perception & Psychophysics, 50*, 225–229.

Pressey, A. W., & Pressey, C. A. (1992). Attentive fields are related to focal and contextual features: A study of Müller-Lyer distortions. *Perception & Psychophysics, 51*, 423–436.

Ramchandran, V. S. (1988). Perceiving shape from shading. *Scientific American*, 259, 76–83.

Ramchandran, V. S., & Anstis, S. M. (1986). The perception of apparent motion. *Scientific American*, May, 102–109.

Ramchandran, V. S., Rao, V. M., & Vidyasagar, T. R. (1973). Apparent movement with subjective contours. *Vision Research, 13*, 1399–1401.

Ratliff, F. (1965). Mach bands: Quantitative studies on neural networks in the retina. New York: Holden-Day.

Rock, I. (1986). The description and analysis of object and event perception. In K. R. Boff, L. Kauffman, & J. P. Thomas (Eds.), *Handbook of perception and human performance. Volume II: Cognitive processes and performance.* New York: John Wiley & Sons.

Rogers, B. J., & Graham, M. (1979). Motion parallax as an independent cue for depth perception. *Perception, 8*, 125–134.

Rubin, E. (1915). *Synoplevde Figurer.* Copenhagen: Gyldendalske.

Schiffman, H. R. (1990) *Sensation and perception: An integrated approach* (3rd ed.). New York: John Wiley & Sons.

Schiffman, H. R. (1996) *Sensation and perception: An integrated approach* (4th ed.). New York: John Wiley & Sons.

Schneider, B., & Parker, S. (1990). Does stimulus context affect loudness or only loudness judgments? *Perception & Psychophysics, 48*, 409–418.

Sekuler, R., & Blake, R. (1994). *Perception* (3rd ed.). New York: McGraw-Hill.

von Senden, M. (1960). *Space and sight: The perception of space and shape in congenitally blind patients before and after operation.* London: Methuen.

Shannon, C. E., & Weaver, W. (1949). *The mathematical theory of communication.* Urbana: University of Illinois Press.

Shepard, R. N., & Zare, S.L. (1983). Path-guided apparent motion. *Science, 220*, 632–634.

Spear, P. D., Penrod, S. D., & Baker, T. B. (1988). *Psychology: Perspectives on behavior.* New York: John Wiley & Sons.

Svaetichin, G. (1956). Spectral response curves of single cones. *Acta Physiologica Scandinavica, 1*, 93–101.

Svaetichin, G., & MacNichol, E. F., Jr. (1958). Retinal mechanisms for achromatic vision. *Annals of the New York Academy of Sciences, 74*, 385–404.

Ternus, J. (1926). Experimentelle Untersuchungen uber phanomenale Identitat. *Psychologische Forschung, 7*, 81–136.

Tynan, P., & Sekuler, R. (1975). Moving visual phantoms: A new contour completion effect. *Science, 188*, 951–952.

Wald, G., & Brown, P. K. (1965). Human color vision and color blindness. *Cold Spring Harbour Symposia on Quantitative Biology, 30*, 345–359.

Wallach, H., & O'Connell, D. N. (1953). The kinetic depth effect. *Journal of Experimental Psychology, 45*, 205–217.

Ware, C., & Cowan, W. B. (1987). Chromatic Mach bands: Behavioral evidence for lateral inhibition in human color vision. *Perception & Psychophysics, 41*, 173–178.

Warren, W. H., Obuseck, C. J., & Acroff, J. M. (1972). Auditory induction of absent sounds. *Science, 176*, 1149.

Weisstein, N., Maguire, W., & Berbaum, K. (1977). A phantom motion aftereffect. *Science, 198*, 955–957.

Wertheimer, M. (1912). Experimentelle Studien uber das Sehen von Bewegung. *Zeitschrift fur Psychologie, 61*, 161–265.

Wever, E. G. (1949). *Theory of hearing.* New York: John Wiley & Sons.

Wright, W. D. (1929). A re-determination of the trichromatic mixture data. *Medical Research Council (Great Britain), Special Report Series, SRS-139*, 1–38.

Index

BROOKS/COLE SOFTWARE REGISTRATION

Thank you for choosing Brooks/Cole software. To qualify for technical support and to be notified about upgrades and new products, please take a moment to complete and return this owner registration card. (This information is for internal use only.)

Name ______________________________

❑ Student ❑ Faculty ❑ Computing Services Administrator

❑ Professional ❑ Other Administrator ❑ Personal

Department ______________________________

Institution/Company ______________________________

Address ______________________________

City/State/ZIP Code ______________________________

Telephone ______________________________

E-mail address ______________________________

Product purchased (include version number) ______________

Date/Place of purchase ______________________________

Equipment on which you will be using this product ___________

Would you be interested in participating in an e-mail discussion group on this product? ______________________

BROOKS/COLE SOFTWARE REGISTRATION

Product purchased (include version number) ______________

____

If you need service, support, or information on our software, please contact our Technical Support Department.

Brooks/Cole Publishing Company
511 Forest Lodge Road
Pacific Grove, California 93950
Telephone: (800) 423-0563 or (800) 214-2661
FAX: (606) 647-5020
E-mail: support@brookscole.com

IMPORTANT:
Keep this portion for your records.
You will need it to receive support.

READ BEFORE OPENING

By breaking the seal on the CD package, you indicate your acceptance of the Brooks/Cole Licensing and Warranty Agreement.

Brooks/Cole Licensing and Warranty Agreement

This is a legal agreement between you, the program user, and Brooks/Cole Publishing Company (Publisher). By installing the software on the enclosed CD-ROM, you are agreeing to the terms of this agreement. If you do not agree to these terms, promptly return this CD-ROM and all accompanying materials.

Grant of License
Brooks/Cole Publishing Company grants you the right to use the enclosed software programs ("Software") on one microcomputer at a time. You may not network the Software or otherwise use it on more than one computer at a time without obtaining a site license from the Publisher. You may not rent, lease, lend, or otherwise distribute copies of the Software to others; however, you may transfer the Software and accompanying materials on a permanent basis, provided you retain no copies and the recipient agrees to the terms of the agreement. For backup purposes, however, you may make one copy of the Software. You may not copy any written materials that accompany the Software.

Copyright
The Software is owned by the Publisher and is protected under the United States and international copyright laws. You must treat the Software as you would any other copyrighted material.

Limited Warranty
The warranty for this CD-ROM is for ninety (90) days. If, during that time period, you find defects in workmanship or material, the Publisher will replace the defective item. The Publisher and Author provide no other warranties, expressed or implied, and shall not be liable for any damages—special, indirect, incidental, consequential, or otherwise. For technical support: call 800-423-0563 or 800-214-2661, fax 606-647-5020, or email support@brookscole.com